It's Not It!

THE MIRACLES OF MIND

It's Not It

THE MIRACLES OF MIND

BY

ANTONIO ALMEIDA

ONE SPIRIT PRESS
PORTLAND, OREGON

© 2012 by Antonio Almeida

All Rights Reserved
Printed in USA

ISBN 978-1893075-21-4
LCCN:2012936578

Cover Design by Ethan Firpo
Interior Design Spirit Press, LLC

This book may not be reproduced in
whole or in part, by electronic or any
other means which exist or
may yet be developed, without
permission of:

One Spirit Press
Portland, Oregon

Dedication

A dedication is a way of demonstrating appreciation to an individual or individuals who have supported the author in many different ways. It is a way to say thanks. I personally have so many people who come to mind, including my parents, my brother and sisters, my son Mark, the many celebrities I have worked with, but most of all, the hundreds of clients who have been my teachers. While guiding them trough their life's challenges- their sharing with me their fears, their setbacks, despair, joys and sadness, and in this I have listened. It was all of you, who pointed me on the path for this book The insights, which now I am sharing here, will help so many others.

I thank everyone, every single person who has come into my life, for just a moment or for a lifetime. I have listened to you and learned the lessons, which I am now sharing with the world. This is your book, heart and lessons. You have helped me rise above the world influences and illusions. This book is the result.

Thank you.

Contents

Introduction	VII
1. Choose Your Place	3
2. The Cause Of Human Failure	9
3. Making A Difference	15
4. Infinite Manifestation	31
5. All Happens As It Should	51
6. Embracing our Differences	65
7. Reality As We Know It	69
8. The Opium of Illusion	77
9. You Are The Paradox	83
10. Self-Love	91
11. Identity	101
12. Healing	109
13. Relationships	117
14. Power	129
15. Creating a Reality	133
16. Responsibility is Freedom	143
17. Destiny	161
Poetic Desire	168
Afterword	173
Colophon	176

Introduction

It's NOT It!

Whether or not you are currently aware, you have arrived here for a reason – a very specific reason, although your specific reason can only be known and understood by you. Consciously you may not be aware of the specific reason that drew you to this book. Rest assured there is one. You have chosen this book, thus we have crossed paths- this has a significant purpose. Every connection we make serves an intention. Every event, condition, and circumstance contains a purpose. This book is about what I know. The information here has the potential to change your life. You are being provided with a choice and an opportunity rolled into one.

What we tell you is already known in your unconscious mind. This book is a trigger and door knock to open your mind. There are no secrets in the Universe. You already know everything there is to know. No one has more access to more knowledge than anyone else.

There is nothing in the Universe but intelligence. You can call IT the Matrix, the fabric, God, Mohammed, Source, or any number of other names. Jesus or Prophets existed before us. They were as us, expressing their views and feelings about a dysfunctional world. They expressed their spirituality, and interpretation of God and Creator. These are names and symbols man has used to have a connection with the Source, Creator, Supreme Being, or Divinity (Intelligence). For thousands of years, we have had a connection with these names. The relationship to Source is triggered when we use these names. In doing so, we communicate with the Source and each other. Most of the world still uses these names and symbols to communicate with what they call or think of as Source.

Whatever images you have or create in your physical world are not IT. That something your mind sees or thinks is God: It's not IT. Can you describe something which is not anything? So, don't describe it! That which is infinite cannot be described or understood by the human mind. That which is infinite can't be something definitive. All there is, is infinite intelligences knowing infinite intelligence.

Whatever you come up with-it's not physical anyway. The science of physics has proven it is Energy. It has no solidity or physical form. This Energy is pure Intelligence. This is a true description; it takes away all physical and visual interpretation thus opening our ability to use our spiritual vision.

A Little Science

All life is constructed of atoms. Within an atom, there is more space than outside of the atom. No matter how solid and physical we look or feel, we, life, are not physical or solid. Our world is a flow of energy, vibrating. Within the atom, there are electrons. Electrons come and go. They can come from a million years in the future and sometimes from the past. Once an electron chooses to leave an atom, it can become an electron in any molecule (a collection of atoms that behave in a certain way). Once an electron is in a molecule it must behave according to the natural law of the molecule.

There is nothing permanent about you. You, me, our world are in constant flux and change. We know that every cell in our body is replaced every 7 years. Some cells are replaced every 7 days. Science tells us the atoms, which were on a beach in Hawaii (as an example) can be in us this minute. Some of the electrons in us come from a million years in the future and some from a very distant past. This constant shifting, coming and going, leaves our heads and minds spinning. The only constant is the idea that life is in a permanent mode of change.

There isn't any separation. The energy does not stop and start, the atoms and molecules don't begin and end. There is a persisting flow of energy as one body and mind. The very shift of electrons shows us life is intelligence based on their ability to choose and not choose.

And the Word was God

We use our physical expression to replay our physical experiences, which are, in fact, illusions. Einstein proved it. We know all form is simply nothingness; neurons and atoms coming together through energy, creating form and experiences by our use of Intelligence. When you take away all the visual and thought associations with IT we become available to Spirit and go beyond thought, our true spiritual nature. This is when we realize the nature of reality and our true-identity is spirit.

Whatever we call our God, Jehovah, or any other name, still it's not IT! These are only names invented by humans for their use. No human thinking and naming or interpretation is true. Human ideas and communication are all based on old ideas and beliefs, which are filled with misperception and myths. Whatever we think or say or call it, it's NOT IT! It is beyond our conceivable understanding. Don't be stuck on a name. Go beyond your traditional thinking.

Names, countries, and tribal groups are all manmade concepts. When in space and looking back you don't see marks on the earth that says 'this is America,' 'this England.' Names are methods of communication created by men. Groups were tribes, geographically separated. It was and still is the vehicle that enables humans to communicate within their tribes (nations). These concepts and religions are still the things which give groups power and, at the same time, separates them from each other.

By having different belief systems we stay separated and divided. These differences are the very things that should unify us, not divide us. The differences are the unknown and the very thing, which brings fear into the human dysfunctional thinking. The non-understanding of each other creates fear instead of what it was meant to create: learning. Don't have blind belief in anything, and this includes the subjects of life. Usually, you would be asked to believe in the authority of someone else. No matter how high the authority, including the bible or any other book, it is still blind belief because you do not know for yourself.

My practice is based on metaphysical principles. Based on these principles, I ask you to find out for yourself. This is unheard of from traditional churches. The church orders you to just follow, believe without question. They tell you it's the law.
Don't believe it!

Antonio Almeida
May 2012
Florida

"Yes, I will try to be. Because I believe that not being is arrogant."

~Antonio Porchia, Voces, 1943, translated from Spanish by W.S. Merwin

"The goal of life is to make your heartbeat match the beat of the Universe, to match your nature with Nature."

~Joseph Campbell

Chapter 1

Choose Your Place

What would you like to see happening to our world and the human race, to your personal life, during your existence, in this lifetime? I would like to experience a new world where all people embrace each other's differences, such as culture, religion, beliefs, and race.

We have created division in many ways by believing we are right and others are wrong. All beliefs are mere expressions of individuality, our sacred gift of freedom of expression. The differences between us make up the totality of the whole. It is the mix together, which makes up the immensity of ONE. And everyone is the missing parts of everyone else. We add to and amplify each other. We all exist for the purpose of acquiring content. It is in learning and acceptance of everything and everyone, which makes you up. This completes us and induces growth. Our awareness, respect, and acceptance of individuality expands our lives, and thus our ability for a more authentic life.

I want to share this inner vision with the hopes it will stimulate your curiosity enough for you to begin to question all of the world teachings, the hand-me-downs, dogmas, and world programming. Just maybe we can begin to create a great new world. This book will be interpreted as controversial by some, and accepted by others that have already immerged above world influences. One thing for sure, you will be thinking and questioning your own beliefs and thoughts ways.

Are you thinking?
This means that you exist.
Who's the thinker behind the thought?

You exist even if you say "I do not exist." The very use of 'I' is an indication of existence. You think therefore you are. You are the thinking, thinking the thought. You are the thinker, thinking the thought.

My hope is you will take responsibility, watch what you choose to believe and question your reality. I personally believe all manmade concepts are not working. They are, in fact, failing miserably. It is time for us to take a look at all these inherent belief systems and begin to create something new, something not based on previous, dysfunctional, and failed concepts. Do not be part of old thinking on topics such as religion, relationships, institutions, governments, or any of these manmade concepts. All of these have, and are made to fail. This book is of a rebellious nature. Its content is set against most belief systems that are frozen in time.

I ask you to believe in nothing outside of yourself. Seek for the answers only within. Allow life to unfold from within you. Be curious about the differences in each human being. Expand your awareness; your curiosity is the doorway to prosperity and an extraordinary life.

We are as unlimited as the Universe. We are an amazing people with so many achievements to be proud of. We have created great masterpieces of music, art, architecture, and lately, amazing technology, which has delivered radical changes in the way we live, and has enabled us to create things which 20 years ago were considered to be impossible. Fifty years ago the global communication network would have been considered a miracle, an impossibility. There is another very real side of our potentiality: we are capable of insanity. We are capable of creating life and at the same time destroying it.

Religions and governments are the powers that are the cause of our division. If you look deeply into the history of all religions, you'll discover below the legalism of religion, they all have one thing in common: One creator, One Source, One entity. They all point out also that our normal way of thinking is dysfunctional, even capable of madness. Our dysfunctional mind believes suffering is necessary. How absurd.

This mind is also reckless and never satisfied. We will do things that ultimately bring us suffering. Whatever we do or may achieve, we will encounter suffering. Our collective human memory is the cause of our thinking, which continues to influence us in our course of destruction. We must change in order to create a new path. Our leaders are the product of our human blueprint, continuing to take us through our repetitive patterns, ignoring the fact we are all united by our spiritual nature.

Pause a minute, take a deep breath, and let go of your old patterns of reading and thinking. Inhale a new reality of compassion and absolute love. Join me in the journey we are taking through consciousness.

CHAPTER ONE — CHOOSE YOUR PLACE

My Choices
Notes

The reason why the world lacks unity, and lies broken and in heaps, is, because man is disunited with himself.

~Ralph Waldo Emerson

Chapter 2

The Cause Of Human Failure

Religion and governments have become our suicide. Dysfunctional living is due to this continuous cycle of mechanical programming, which is the blueprint that activates our human experiences. We use the same content our ancestors have used since the beginning of time. The mind-content makes up our lives and we continuing repeating the same mistakes, same fears, same experiences, in different times. They may seem different, but they are not. It appears we have evolved because we have made our lives faster, easier, and more pleasurable, but suffering, pain and hatred is still prominent this day, with one difference: the numbers have expanded.

I ask the questions: Why are we still divided? Why is it we are still afraid of our differences? Can you see the illusion? The drama and the stories, you create. Just because I think differently, have a different opinion, speak a different language, and I am of a different color- I am of our planet, our home and I am of the same specie origin. We are of one soul.

It is ignorance, which places people in a place of fear and believing someone else is the chosen and has power over the rest. There is now a recognition no one is above the other, we all have the same rights and the nations belong to us, the people. Not just one, but all are co-owners. Countries belong to all people. Not just one, not just some, but all people. No one person or country can own the planet or a piece of it. At the very most, we are given a stewardship to take care of that which we use. Our home on this planet is for us all. None of us have more spirit or rights than another. Power is a joke. The only power anyone has is what we allow them to have.

Fear is not the opposite of love. Like love, it is an acceptance, albeit to a lesser degree. A room full of light can have a dark corner or closet. This darkness does not make it less a part of the room, it is just not as visible. This is the same with love and fear. Love is always there just not as visible.

People are kept without education and without access to the knowledge of what is happening in their world. Who is the 'them?' It is us. We are kept in captivity by the tyrants and greedy by

Chapter Two — The Cause of Human Failure

virtue of our own asleepness. Look at the images from all over the world: at Egypt, India, and Africa. Children living in the worst conditions: dirty, barefoot, and hungry. Look at the situations in Kenyan and Somalian refugee camps, where thirty thousand children are dying every month from hunger, while the ones in power are swimming in luxury and have riches beyond imagination. Look at past history of Germany, when Hitler brainwashed the German children to love him more than their own parents and these children grew up to give their lives to this monster. This type of brain washing goes on all over the world: in the Muslim world, the White Supremacists in America, and of course the lost children in Africa who are conscripted into fighting as soon as they can carry a weapon.

Look at what we are still allowing. Why are we still allowing ignorance to prevail? Do not believe some have authority over you or they will have you serve them as if they were ordained by God. They want you to believe the lies so you will follow them blindly. The flourishing of terrorism is due to ignorance and poverty. War should be fought against ignorance. Abolish ignorance and we will abolish war. If we create a new ideology that has its basis in spirituality, we will cure all human diseases and bring about unity.

Most of our advancements have been merely for selfish means, done regardless of the damage we leave behind. By tracing back to the beginning of the human race you will discover even though we have advanced by leaps and bounds our habits are still the same and our concepts have not changed at all. In the beginning, there were tribes; today, governments. One group, afraid of another, generated control to assure its means of survival.

This is religion: the invention of words and taboos, thereby inducing fear through force or superstition. Those who create these concepts and Gods create them for themselves to assure their position of power and leadership, producing today's chiefs, presidents and kings. Riding the wave of fear and ignorance, they claim power to rule the others. Seducing and manipulating the others in order to protect and preserve their places-to become like Gods themselves.

Tribal chiefs, preachers, leaders, kings, presidents and other religious leaders; they elect their own in order to protect their places of power and control. The struggle for survival was and is still the motivation of these to invent many ways of manipulating the lower and less mentally evolved, today's social structures. Again, it is fear. which feeds this illusion and by recognizing this insanity, we can shift the course of our lives and the lives of everyone on this planet.

All worldly concepts are manmade: made for

CHAPTER TWO   THE CAUSE OF HUMAN FAILURE

man, not God. Religions are manmade not God-made. Governments are manmade, but not for the people. They are for organized groups to control their wealth and power. We are to live our lives as if everyone else were us. As if we are taking the same journey as everyone else. No one stays behind. You have the rights to your own views. This book is meant to celebrate our human connectivity. In the world there are many views, many personalities, many beliefs. I welcome all of them.

The man who never alters his opinion is like standing water, and breeds reptiles of the mind.

~William Blake

Chapter 3

Making A Difference

Can one person make a difference in her or his lifetime? Will you die before you have a chance to make a difference? I believe it only takes one to influence a change. Many have come, many have gone, and we have changed because they expressed their beliefs and got involved. We all have been touched by their messages and actions. But have we changed for the better? I believe that we have discovered the hidden secrets of Nature, and we are able to change it to fit our needs, but our course of destruction we have not changed.

Change The Great Consciousness/Work The Consciousness Shift

Change is perhaps the scariest word in the English language. For years, advertisers have known this and avoided the word. Perhaps it is scary because change represents what we don't know. Yet in the Universe as we know it, the only true constant is change. Even as you sit and read this you are changing, electrons are passing in and out of your body and environment, your understanding is changing the very perception you hold at this moment.

What you are today, you were yesterday and what you will be tomorrow, you are today. Consciousness follows you. You are your consciousness. There is no magic moment of waking up and seeing everything has changed. Like any other desire in our life we must take some kind of action if we want to bring about change, experience true bliss and connection in life. A body or mind at rest tends to stay at rest. Action, even small steps, gets you to the next place in your soul journey.

You can't make radical changes in the patterns of your life until you begin to see yourself exactly as you are right now. Once you have seen how you are interacting with your reality and the patterns in your life, change can happen. It happens without effort. The problem most of us encounter is our ego gets in the way and tries to keep us from seeing how we are behaving and interacting.

To get to the point of real insight is not an easy task. You must be able to see yourself how you are without judgments, illusion and resistance. As you gain insight, you gain understanding. Understanding produces compassion, tolerance, and flexibility. You can understand others because you have begun to understand yourself. On the soul journey we all take, our ultimate understanding is of our self. As we understand our self, accept our humanity, and failings without judgment, we learn uncritical love or unconditional love. Absolute love is our goal. When we accept all life as the same, when we see none of us have more Truth, love, or divinity than another, when we embrace all humanity as our brothers we are on a path that is healing and change will be a true wonderment.

TRANSFORMATION

Inherent in transformation is release and freedom. In the process of consciousness work or meditation, personal transformation takes place. How you begin is definitely different than how you are when the work or meditation is concluded. Consciousness work and meditation sensitize and make you more aware of your thoughts and actions. Anyone who starts consciousness work, meditation or any other soul journey must expect change. Something in your life is asking for you to change, to transform how you see things how you think and how you act.

Perhaps change is the wrong word, for what happens is less of a change and more of a revelation of self. It is like peeling of layers of dirt from a wonderful painting you begin to see the true self the I AM I. Layers of arrogance, antagonism, and anxiety are washed away. In the real self you find stillness, quietness, and calm; a radiant self ready to meet the existence of your humanity. Because in consciousness work and meditation you must remain present, tensions disappear, fear, and restlessness fade, passions and desires for worldly things recede.

As you peel back the layers of the subconscious and become aware of the mechanical motives you have been functioning under, a new world of real thinking, straight thinking, in the abstract appears; your intuition is profoundly awakened. Your mind clarifies, allowing you to see things and use knowledge in reality without prejudice and illusion. Transformation and change are conscious choices we all most make on the journey we take.

The Ring of Fire

When we speak of change, we are not speaking of changing a hairstyle, self-esteem, or even changing our ability to love. We are talking about changing the very core of our being. Through consciousness work and meditation, the very nature of our nervous system changes how it reacts and interacts with our reality. This transformation is often seen as a glow on the being of person. Often radiance is present. This work is the beginning of the ability to manifest in your life that which is needed. The involuntary becomes voluntary. Through focus, and staying present you begin what is often called the crucible of fire, the burning away of what is not needed.

In the work you begin to see a natural order of consciousness. You gain faith. Not faith because you believe something to be so, but faith in the function of principle and beingness. You gain faith of something being true because you have experienced it in a heightened state of awareness. In the fire of transformation, all that is not reality of truth is burnt away. A natural morality is formed in the fire. A morality of understanding and tolerance is born and revealed to you. This is not an outer morality or a code of behavior imposed by a church or society, but rather an inner sense of direction. In the fire of transformation you are tempered and your true being is revealed by the burning away of false roles, and a million years of beliefs that keep you locked into a system of pain, anguish, and suffering.

The Razor's Edge

There comes a point in our consciousness work where we are faced with some ultimate choices. We come to the edge of the cliff and see below the wonderful cool waters. Our pain is great, our life without purpose at that moment, and we must make a choice. We must choose to die or live. Sometimes this choice is symbolic but it is, never the less, a choice we each make. The transformation from unconscious living into consciousness aware of consciousness takes courage. For the ego this is death, real death and we must be able to accept this death with fearlessness and conviction. This time usually comes when the pain in our lives is so great we must do something.

As we stand on the razor's edge of the cliff, we must face the purpose of our life and existence. Our identity as human, mother, father, sister, or brother has been shattered. Our life as we envisioned it no longer exists. As we stand with our heart perhaps broken, and in our soul no joy, no wanting life, to continue we must decide. At this moment we are at a point of real decision, perhaps the first real decision we have ever made in our life. Below the cliff the cooling waters have turned into a raging fire. The fire of transformation will burn away all illusions and delusions. We, ego, will no longer exist and there is no vision of what is to be. In this moment, we must take a leap of faith. Faith not based on beliefs, but a knowing this leap is a leap all conscious beings must take.

There is no hand of God to catch you and no one can make it easier or push you. No one knows what you will be like when you arise from the fires of transformation. When the insanity can no longer be born by mortal being we must, like all those who have awoken before us, know consciousness aware of consciousness, I AM I, is our only identity and our only manifested purpose. When the fires have burnt away the false identity you are finally left with that which is so about your existence: I AM I. There is no greater joy, or peace or bliss in life than this experience of the true self. This I AM I that we speak of is not limited to any religion or way of thinking but is the great inheritance all humanity shares.

Perpetual Change

Change in our life does not stop. Everything changes. If there is one constant in the Universe it is change. The essence of our experience on this planet is change. There is a constant flow of change in our consciousness. Even in a vegetative state, we are changing. Every moment is different. Every moment is changed from the last. You can't hold onto the past, or even the future, because change is always in process. We spend our lives categorizing the experience of changes that come into our experience. We give them labels of good, bad, or neutral. Once we have categorized them, we spend the rest of the time running from the bad, trying to find the good, and ignoring the neutral experiences we find boring.

Inherent in change is a power: a power to bring

about a heightened state of awareness. When we stay focused on the present moment, we flow with the experience and embrace consciousness as it is. We grow old not because of some genetic quirk, but because we focus on the past and how we were. We try to freeze-frame our consciousness and being in a state that was only momentary. Our bodies stiffen when we have frozen into a state of existence that is only a picture in a memory, and like all still pictures we cannot move. Conscious life is about movement. Consciousness does not stay still; insight is fleeting and yesterday's understanding gives way for today's realization. Happiness is transitory, life is fleeting, but I AM I is forever. It is an endless state of experiencing the unfolding of mind in its infinite variety.

The work, our work as consciousness/beingness, is simple: it is about insight and awareness. Meditation as presented in this series is simply a pathway for insightful awareness. Bliss, happiness, and peace are by-products of embracing the I AM I nature of reality. Physical life is transitory, but consciousness is without beginning or end.

Leap Into Sanity

Prophets and seers have warned us of our destructive ways. They said, 'look how you live, see what you are doing, the suffering you have created.' They pointed to a possibility for change and yet the collective nightmare of our destructive ways continues. The world was not ready for them, yet they produced an effect of vital, necessary awakening.

Their teachings pointed the way out of the collective insanity. The teachings are simple and easy to understand, but the messages have become distorted and misinterpreted. Leaders of society have prosecuted these spiritual teachers, and even killed them, because of their views and teachings. They changed and manipulated the messages to fit a particular group. Religions have become a reason for division rather than unification. Instead of bringing about an end to violence and hatred and the realization all beings are united by one common goal, they brought more violence and hatred. They all claim to be right while others are false, thus creating more separation by defining themselves by their differences.

Standing on the cliff of destruction, it is our choice to leap the great chasm of insanity into the arms of sanity. It is a scary leap. We must leave our old beliefs, ideals, greed, and desire behind us. We must know at the moment we let go of our ego-centered life, a new way will be presented to us. We reside in a realm of no power. The secret is sanity is the ultimate power. No amount of wealth, or beauty, can give you power. Clinging to our old beliefs, we remain subject to insanity.

Breathe

Breathe in deeply. Survey all of the insanity, pain, and confusion you carry within you. With each breathe; allow this to flow from you. Feel yourself centered. As the flow of air leaves you, let go of the torment of desire. Allow yourself to be.

Repeat this surveying within all that holds you from your true inheritance as a child of the Universe. Know you are the thought of the creator-source and you are the creator creating the thought. You are connected to all life; forever whole, complete, and perfect. The essence of you has no beginning nor end. Allow yourself, in this one moment, to be embraced by the entire Universe and experience the totality of the all-being.

When We are Two and Not One

In the history of our world, we have often been divided. There has always been us and the others. The us has usually been patriarchal (domineering males in power), the other females and slaves. Since early civilization, this has dominated our global thinking. The duality created by this type of thinking has produced a split in our psyche; divisions in the universal unconsciousness, making us believe that there are some who have more power, divinity, wealth, and ability.

This division has generated an atmosphere of fear and persecution carried through in governments, churches, schools, and families thorough the world. This misunderstanding of the nature of reality, the division creates animosity, idols, and insanity. As a species, we side with those we think have power.

Refuse the Bitter Pills

The Ketman effect comes into play when those in a position to change the course of history, by positive assertion of Truth and premises based on Truth. Yet these same leaders deny what is right out of fear and lack of courage. Simply put, the act of covering one's behind rather than take a stand for what is right for all people. Living with contradictions has become a way of life for intelligent people. With Ketman-like qualifications, leaders assert they have the right to be wrong. Being wrong is more than just aligning oneself with a mistake; it joins the delusion of a democracy and expressions of duality. Our human past is replete with revolutions born out of Ketman-like silence.

Refusing to be responsible is opium to the ego-driven mind. Intelligent leaders are swept up in the euphoria and end up being mediocre in their willingness to shout out for what is right. Why are we willing to sacrifice our sense of justice and equality for all, for this illusion and euphoria of being mediocre? What kind of pill have we been swallowing to allow our country and world get to this state of consciousness? While we criticize another country for their incarceration of individuals for their need to express themselves, we vote in politicians who would limit our freedoms. We vote in those who tell us our freedoms are limited to their narrow view of life.

We hear politicians tell us those who are homosexual are not of God. What is next? Will we vote these idiots into office and watch while they tell us those who practice learning another language, reading a book, or producing a painting are not of God? This is not as far fetched as you might think. Historically, a lack of support for the arts and languages is the path that dictators take.

The question remains: why are intelligent people willing to stand behind a premise that is foul and destructive? How does one live with a contradiction; knowing the Truth and yet willing to live the lie? Searching through all I can, I am stupefied by this willingness to accept erroneous beliefs, except for one small idea. We have lost our courage and pioneering spirit, becoming complacent in our convictions, and willing to side with erroneous beliefs.

Forget about the red and yellow peril of the past generations and look at what we are constructing. We are a peril to the very health of what democracy stands for. We have decided equal is treating everyone the same rather than celebrating the individuality of being. We have decided we know what is of God/Truth. Our policy is no longer one of embracing the huddled masses, but of exclusion and persecution.

The courage to be takes us out of the illusion of the ordinary and into an extraordinary state of existence. Our lives become one of embracing individuality and yet understanding the core of all life is of one idea, no matter what it is called. Those with courage of being don't have to spout their passion, they live it. They are willing to stand up in the face of adversity for what is Truth and right for all. Those with the courage to be, protect children from the rhetoric of fear and the opium of delusion. Individuality becomes a source of pride and celebration. Freedom for all is the major premise of governing law.

The courage to be is more than accepting Truth, it is about freeing our minds from the captivity of the delusion of freedom and ego. As long as our intellects remain captive we will cover our behinds and invoke the Ketman aspect of consciousness. To become courageous, refuse to swallow the bitter pills we are handed and stand up to those who would pervert our freedom and feed us false premises.

Have the courage to be as you were created. Learn to be Truth expressing in infinite variety undefined by boundaries of false beliefs. Embrace life outside of predictable outcomes. If we do this together we will find the courage to continue. Hold my hand and join me in our embracing the Truth.

"Being is our purpose and the moment contains everything. The distinction between past, present, and future is only a stubbornly persistent illusion."
-Albert Einstein

CHAPTER THREE — MAKING A DIFFERENCE

Ways I Can Make A Difference
Notes

"I'm not different for the sake of being different, only for the desperate sake of being myself. I can't join your gang: you'd think I was a phony and I'd know it."

~Vivian Stanshall

Chapter 4

Infinite Manifestation

It's Ok To Have A Different Belief System!

It's ok to have a different belief system! It's not ok to condemn another because their beliefs are different! We, the people of the world, should hold the leaders responsible to bring us together by condemning ignorance. First, educate. Abolish ignorance!

The History

Six thousand years ago leadership was about the survival of the body and people. Leaders were the persons in the tribe or nation who could best ensure physical survival. They probably understood growing and hunting better than anyone else in the tribe. The rules and laws were about survival.

Many of the religious rules practiced today have their roots in this mode of leadership. To quote Mary Ritley, Ph.D., "What is necessary for survival becomes sacred."

LEADERSHIP

All of us, no matter what nationality, have responsibilities as citizens. We are, first of all, responsible to our selves and family to make sure we have all of the basics of survival and life; then we have a duty to our schools, to do the very best we can do, to study diligently, use discipline and take the gift of knowledge to our hearts.

Finally, we have a duty to our country. The investment in education is not just about becoming a businessman or woman and making money. We have a duty to our countries to use education to improve the lives of all people in all countries. Every child in every country has the right to food, water, shelter, safe passage, and education. In the world today, we have millions of children who have none of these. The basic needs of humanity are not being met. It is up to you and I to use our creative minds, and our leadership abilities, to solve these world problems. To solve world problems, we start in our motherlands.

Education is about creative leadership. It is about bringing a bright future of peace and gentleness to all people.

CHAPTER FOUR   INFINITE MANIFESTATION

~~~~~~~~~~~~~~~~~~~~~~~~~~~~~~~~~~

DID YOU KNOW?

Leadership is an issue that affects us all, globally and locally. We cannot afford to turn our heads and say we are not impacted by a lack of authentic leadership. Each of us is called upon to exercise leadership in many ways. Be it leading a government or business, guiding the young minds of children and young adults, leading a family, standing for what is right, organizing a social event, or taking children to school or a household, we are called on again and again to play leadership roles. We are each propelled into being custodians and stewards of what is right and good, human and of lasting value, for those in our care.

Did you know there are nine million six hundred and ninety thousand religions in the world? Just look it up. As you can see, diversity is not the problem. No matter how you are different, no matter how you express it, just like the different stars in the sky, the different galaxies in the Universe, there is only one Mind (God) and our different views and beliefs are the mix of the immensity of ONE. The problem is that most are ignorant that the root of our continuous cycle of discord, division, and separation is just us. We must take responsibility, collectively and individually.

Leadership is an attitude—a state of being—a way of looking at the world.

A leader maintains the vision and faith in those ideals, beliefs, and hopes while living those values as a model and example for others to follow. It means raising the sights and holding the focus of those, we lead in such a way they are empowered to reach their potentials. It means enabling people by getting the roadblocks out of their way and often out of their thinking. To do this, of course, the leader must grasp the larger picture at all times and hold the course for the benefit of all. A leader defines reality for those who follow.

"The first responsibility of a leader is to define reality. The last is to say thank you. In between, the leader is a servant."
— Max DePree

Cooperate or Die

Cooperation is the way our species has survived. The very cells in our body survive through cooperation. Peace does not come because we are at war; it does not happen by keeping the majority of our world citizenry uneducated, hungry, and ill. When we cooperate as countries as a world we secure the future of our children and citizens.

Our ability to affect the outcomes of our world is within our grasp. The simplicity of small steps is available to all of us. By teaching our children peaceful existence, making sure all children have access to education and health care as well as food, safe water, and opportunity, we become authentic leaders.

Future of Leadership

Government's role in a democracy is not to produce business and wealth for a few. Its role is leadership. A leader in a government needs to be strong, exemplify compassion, and carry a vision of a better world. When governments focus on creating business rather than leading, the individual is left out of the equation. Our history as a people is filled with examples of great leaders who lead through compassion and peaceful co-operation.

Skills

I believe these skill are within the grasp of all individuals. When we exercise them we secure the future in this NOW moment.

Critical thinking skills• Creativity in thinking and approaches • The ability to think straight in the abstract. • To remain objective under pressure and effectively use information • Practice honesty and ethical behavior • Excellent communication skills • Compassion for those lead. •An ability to think and act globally. This means the skill to see how each decision produces a action and result that is felt in a our global community. • A true understanding the whole is greater than the sum of its parts. • The ability to see all people have the same needs for food, air, shelter, safety, love, self esteem, learning, and purpose. These needs are the bonds of being human. All children, no matter what their race or religion or political beliefs have the inalienable right to grow up free from harm of war and famine.

No matter what the country, the color of our skin and eyes, at the core of our being we are the same. We are human beings who are aware of our selves and our ability to think and reason. This is called consciousness. At the core of our being we are consciousness. Just as each of us holds this consciousness so do each of us hold the ability to be leaders at some level.

Learning the Craft

Leadership like any other skill can be learned. It is learned by practice and discipline. We need leaders who are willing to become excellent. The world needs leaders who are willing to go the extra mile to be extraordinary in their leadership practice.

People see leaders as role models. They look at a leader as one who can help them obtain the deep human satisfaction they crave from their life and work. They will continue to give their loyalty only as long as the leader keeps proving that he is able to show the way to these satisfactions.

Being a leader means you have the power to shape and mold the present and future of people's lives, of an organization through cooperation of the group. An authentic leader does not deal with luck but with intelligent organization, delegation, empowering his followers to be leaders, charisma, and a basic understanding of the nature of humankind: the needs, wants, and longing of people on both a conscious and unconscious level.

The authentic leaders have some recognizable characteristic and abilities which make them stand out from the crowd. Some of the traits are innate, and some can be learned. Think of them as skills. Here is a leadership profile:

AUTHENTIC LEADERS:

- Have the ability to recognize weaknesses and strengths in oneself and others
- The ability to set goals and to meet them
- The ability to pass credit onto others for their personal contributions
- The ability to accept personal responsibility
- The ability to find and use the right resource to accomplish a task
- The ability to measure the degree of success and failure
- The ability to understand the use of power

- The ability to turn every situation into a learning experience.
- The ability to accept a position of power without undue reluctance or zeal
- The ability to have a driving force towards personal achievements without being self-centered or greedy
- The ability to deal with the present in a realistic manner, while dreaming and planning future accomplishments
- The ability to maintain a balance between the physical, spiritual and emotional sides of one's life
- The ability to plan projects and goals so they produce a better life for all concerned
- The ability to understand the way a situation is handled is even more important than factual information in achieving good results
- The constant drive to know and understand more about everything
- The ability to discriminate between truth, wishful thinking and the hard facts
- The ability to understand one's goals and desires are often more complex than those one is leading
- The ability to awaken those around them to an understanding of their true potential

And some most important skills:

- An authentic leader has the ability to look at his followers eye to eye and say thank you for their loyalty

- The ability to work side-by-side followers when necessary

The reality of it is you are a leader whether you want to be or not. The only difference between people is their sphere of leadership. A parent is a leader to his children, a teacher to the students, student to his peers and siblings, and of course, a manager to his employees.

Although the realm of your leadership may be different from others, the qualities demanded of a leader are the same. Each of us has an opportunity to coach or assist different amounts of people. No matter how many in your following it is important to develop leadership skills. The study of leadership is not scientific it is philosophical and psychological in nature.

Leadership is not about being charismatic nor is it about having power. Leadership is about helping others obtain their purpose in life and leaving this earth in better shape than it was when you were born.

Taking Responsibility: Where to Start

We allow the ones in power to stay in power. We created them and the situation is us. Stop following the idols and the images you mimic. Your source of life is not an idol, nor image, nor person. It is not a saint, Prophet, or person that will save us. It is me, it is you. We are all collectively one. All of one.

We have created the leaders, and the religions. They come from us. They are expressions of our hopes and fears. We carry within ourselves our human memory, the history of all human civilization. Our reference points are the content and memory that is embedded in our psyche. Our physical memory carries all of our fears and hate. It is an illusion! We can create a new thinking by erasing old memories that have no place in the present.

The New And Evolved

We can create a new world out of the confusion! A new consciousness is arising. Pay attention, because it is happening. This change is called enlightenment. This is due to a merging of philosophies, wisdoms, and teachings. The West meets East. It teaches us if we let go of identification with the past-- let go of the dogmas, the superstitions-- we will discover that there are no secrets. We have hidden within our deepest self the limitlessness of creation itself. This has nothing to do with how spiritual you are, or what you believe, but everything to do with your state of consciousness.

I believe a very big part of the world population has already discovered and is recognizing that humanity is now faced with the biggest challenge of all time. We have to make immediate choices.

Evolve Or Die

A rapidly growing percentage of the global population is already experiencing their own spiritual transformation and evolving out of old ways of thinking. Old, manmade concepts are fast vanishing and the immergence of a new belief system is fast coming; a deeper understanding going beyond thought, deeper than consciousness, and beyond the egoist mind set. Hidden in the inner being is the answer: there is one Mind, one Source.

We must trust the Universe to be happy, prosperous, and well.

Situations are now unfolding all over the world and the conditions we are experiencing are our responsibility. God is not responsible for our conditions, we are. Our thoughts, beliefs, and actions shape our world. Regardless of your current religious preference or lack thereof, you should investigate and question your position in the life of your world by adopting a strong belief that you are consciously creating your life.

Our time on this planet must have a definite

purpose: to build our lives with full consciousness of only the present. What are you doing now? What is now? Only this moment is real.

Control The Ego

Our ego is built out of beliefs, fears, and our need to survive. Our ego thinks to survive we need to be greedy making sure we have all that is needed. Gandhi stated it very clear when he said, "Even Christ must speak in the language of bread when the people are hungry." Unless we see that our individual survival is connected to each other and when one of us is starving we all starve. To control the ego is to learn to let go of the survival dynamic as our ego sees it.

You control your ego when:

You learn to recognize it is acting out of fear.
You recognize you are being greedy.
You are playing a role rather than being authentic.

Learn to be self observant. By watching yourself interact, you learn when you are knee-jerking to the will of your ego. It is the ego we need to conquer, not each other or the oceans. Define your values and respect others.

Chapter Four — Infinite Manifestation

The Immergence Of A New Consciousness

The way of the future is already happening. The immergence of a new consciousness is sweeping our planet. Our technological breakthroughs can be used for good or malice. This *new way* of communication is not new. Alchemists, seers, prophets, and psychics have been able to communicate for centuries without devices. We are faced with a radical crisis threatening the survival of all humans on this planet. This is the result of the human-egoist-dysfunctional mind. This disease has been pointed out by enchanted teachers, prophets, and seers for thousands of years. Now, for the first time, our dysfunctional ways are threatening our own survival and the survival of our mother Earth. A transformation of the human mind is vital. The old ways don't apply. Old men who are frozen in time are in control of our lives and holding us hostage.

The violence that we are experiencing all over the world is the cause of greed and of power hungry few. They are not interested in the good of God or country. They will have their own people killed to protect their fortunes, even discarding the future of their own children. The root of evil is vested self-interest. Government is not the solution. The interests of the few will not serve the needs of the masses, but only create a mirage in order to drain their energy.

Ignore this mirrored illusion and seek inside. Seek to join energies with others. The power, which each of us possesses to tap into the Universal Mind, if united, can be a force for good, and an unstoppable one. There is a huge consciousness through which we are all linked. Through the web of humanity, we can unite the consciousness of our planet.

Start today, through my web site (www.spiritualsite.com). You are invited. Help is available. Join with the family of man to start addressing our common concerns on a global level. The greed of the ones in power is the cause of poverty and the suffering of the majority of world's population. This is also a cause for the masses to rise up and invent ways to protect each other and survive. There is a shift in human consciousness, which now is rising making it impossible for the return of the old ways.

World Awakening

Success depends on a shift in human consciousness. The greatest human achievements are not works of science, art, and technology,. The greatest human achievement is humanity recognizing the miracle of one source. Through recognition of our mistakes and the awakening of the dimension within us, we can rise above thought and come in touch with our spirituality.

We are collectively responsible for the world's

Chapter Four — Infinite Manifestation

situation and individually, in our daily actions, we are responsible for the way we interact with each other. The biggest impact on our planet has been due to humanity, to our constant craving for comfort and for the things that provide us pleasure and status.

We have invented a million ways to make life as easy as possible. There is nothing wrong with having and wanting these things. What is wrong is we have done it with no regard to how we affect others and rape our planet. We continue to invest in all possible ways to acquire more. We have gone as far as losing our own identity and placing our identity with the things we possess.

Through commercialism, we feel lost without our brands. If the things you identify with are taken away, who would you be? Is the I am Prada, Rolex, Mercedes, or your status? Who would you be if all of your material possessions were taken away? Whatever you identify with, does it give you a sense of self? If so, I advise you to investigate your thinking and see how your life is being influenced by this identification with temporal things. When some people loose all of their possessions, or even family members, they lfind that their sense of fear gives away to deep peace, serenity, and complete freedom from fear.

In the face of all of this, how can it be that they

feel such peace? When you have nothing to identify with, who are you then? I believe that it is in this state that you truly identify with the self. It is in this state you are the 'I AM' -- you are Consciousness through which everything is known. It is then that you are conscious of consciousness itself—it is the peace of God, the ultimate truth of who you are, the 'I AM.'

It may seem that I have steered away from the core of the book—Let me assure you that, in fact, I am getting right to the point. You continue blaming everything and everyone for our troubles and the troubles of the world, but we are all responsible. The change must begin right where you stand.

The Beginning

In the study of evolution and the development of human knowledge, we have unveiled the origin of life. Science has given us the realization we are surrounded by pure intelligence (energy). All form, meaning everything that exists, seen or unseen, such as nature, color, wind, sounds, emotion, our physical bodies, planets, everything. Everything that exists is the result of invisible energy.

The survival dynamic in us causes a preoccupation of having more and more. We want bigger houses, more clothes, more cars, more and more and more. Our ego has taught us that to survive we must have more. The reality is that cooperation is the key to survival, not acquiring more of anything. Longing to understand our true nature, we misidentify with the physical life around us. Our cries in the middle of the night for something greater than ourselves are only answered by exploration of our inner abilities. We forget to explore our own inner abilities to acquire the spiritual gifts of our divine inheritance. They are what will connect us on the dimension of oneness.

Trace back to our coming into the world and you are able to see why we do what we do. We all have gone through the same process: Out of our mother's womb, our eyes open to the world around us and our mechanical experiences begin. Programming starts: our senses capture sounds, touch, color, heat, cold, speech. The physical world is seductive. It produces attachments. Soon, the collective unconscious, the race inheritance memories, and the ongoing experiences begin to negatively synergize in our minds. The teachings of our parents, rules and the influences of our environment cause us to disconnect from our source. Our separation from pure intelligence (pure energy) takes place. Our senses trick us into forgetting our true source of being.

Now, the distraction of the world is in its allure.

In the world, you are now exposed to the voices of authorities, the media, books, products, culture, environment-- all of this content fills our minds. The spiritual plane is something you feel intuitively. We sense something inside that tells us that we are timeless, invincible, and perfect.

The world programming has already taken hold. We are distracted, trying to fulfill our physical cravings and at the same time, trying to decipher what our purpose is. Religions and world teachings are steering you away from the source, and by adopting these teachings, we have lost our connectivity with each other. Our nature, the inner craving to love and be loved, drives us to become the prey of opinions, manipulation, and belief systems from outside influences. We begin to create our lives out of our experiences and memories. We cling to one another so that we can see ourselves, through each other, unconscious but gravitating towards love and belonging, which is our nature.

Our ego centered consciousness creates time, isolation, and suspicion. These states of consciousness create separation. The cycle of our earthly lives leaves us void of meaning and purpose. We live out in an existential void, trying to fill our craving for meaning and purpose with greed, obsessiveness, and the struggle for personal power. We live this limited life, never accepting our extraordinary, unlimited potential. All energies are spent on providing and preserving our physical existence. We created time, which becomes the prison of our spirit. Our sense of time is fashioned from our memories and experiences, our ego, our self-made prison.

Memories, experiences, and thoughts become our prison, keeping us away from spirit and unavailable to the present. Living in a world that is deadened by physical distractions and enticements, plus the influences they create, we fill our lives with obsessions and objects that blind us to what goes on inside of us. We remain ignorant of our divinity and potential infinite splendor.

Come and join me! Be a light, a splendor unto the world so our light may fall on the Truth and wipe out the pain and ignorance. Do you hear your splendor calling you?

"Chance is a word void of sense; nothing can exist without a cause."

~Voltaire

Chapter 5

All Happens As It Should

Everything that happens in the world and in our lives is not by chance. Science can explain how our world came into existence, starting with the aspects of world events and the circumstances of our lives. In 1925, Albert Einstein revealed to the world the scientific evidence proving matter is energy. These atoms are composed of sub particles that collide and become pure energy. At the time, Einstein believed what he had discovered, these particles of energy were also intelligent. Everything is energy and intelligence at some level.

Electrons come and go into atoms. When the electrons leave the atom they have the ability to choose which atom, they join. But once they join an atom and a molecule they must act/behave according to the axiomatic law governing this atom in that molecule. We know atoms are changing and traveling all the time. An electron (or atom) from the beach of Hawaii could be in you this very minute. We are told electrons can travel from billions of years in the past or future. They don't seem to be limited by the sense of human time.

Everything that exists in the Universe which we experience with our senses –from the infinitely large to the infinitely small– goes far beyond the theory that what we see as solid is actually subatomic particles creating form by way of gravity. The bottom line is Einstein discovered all things, broken down to their most basic form, consist of the same stuff. This stuff is what we are made of. In other words, everything, including you and me, are in the mix of the soup making up the Universe.

Just as an individual drop of water is not the ocean, but has the same properties as the ocean, we are not the Universe, but we have what IT has. To the physical senses, all appears solid, but everything is made up of subatomic particles, vibrating at different frequencies, making up different forms, and all are made up of the same pure energy. Anything and everything, which exists, the universe, when broken down into its purest and most basic form and analyzed by science is made up of vibrating frequencies of energy. When this energy collides with other frequencies it forms what we experience in our reality. The result determines what we experience in our lives and in the world. For proof, you should look up Einstein, Newton, and other scientists. The number one reason for the problems of our world is ignorance.

Regardless of what religion you practice or believe in, we must begin to construct a foundation where people can create lives of freedom. Freedom will be realized when people are able to have their needs met and can bridge the gap of their separation from others. We have seen the rhetoric of different religions. They are like the different languages on our planet. The differences are not at the core of the religion. It is only at the surface or the legalism of the religion. By looking deeper and with an open mind you will discover the hidden truths have been there all along. This knowledge will arm you and the facts will manifest as miracles in your own life.

What physics has proven is only the icing-on -the-cake. In fact, one of the greatest discoveries, brought about by spiritual seekers, enlightened teachers, is the truth of our human connection: we are all ONE. If we are in this world together, then why are we not yet functioning together? We are one and as such we are also energy, thus creating events and situations in our world. If we are one, we are of one mind, one intelligence and we must have knowledge of our thoughts.

Knowing that our thoughts are energy, then these thoughts must create other thoughts, which travel into the empty field, space. This field is full of other energies that attract to each other the same, and then create other thoughts, then on and on to infinity. This brings into reality experiences, events, situations, and form. If our thoughts are in harmony with other positive energies, belief systems that gather strength by merging with Universal energy, we can directly influence our world, create and experience whatever we choose to experience.

We have power over our lives. This means we must individually and as a whole take responsibility in creating our world. A handful of scientists have known of this powerful fact: we are of one and thus we are the creators of our experiences. The help you are seeking, will not come from outside. There is no old wise man with a long white beard who will come to save the world.

We have chosen to believe our dysfunctional human mind, thus we continue to create a dysfunctional world. We create devices to communicate with each other across the globe at the speed of light and yet we have not grasped at the fact, we can also create a world of plenty. A world of harmony, love, and peace, where all differences are welcome and necessary for our own growth. Science continues to try to solve the mysteries of the Universe and Nature, but it cannot because we are part of the mystery, we are trying to solve.

Regardless of how much of this you believe or understand, your life experiences are the result of your thoughts, actions, and beliefs. In fact, your life and everything in it and even the entire world is the result of consciousness and it will happen precisely as you believe it will.

It has been proven that there is a law of cause and effect, and this law is infinite and it is not singular. This means everyone, regardless of who you are, the same law works for all and through all. It has been proven: our thoughts have creative power and we cause our mind to do definite things for and through us. Mind responds to the whole as well as to individuals. Mind, our collective consciousness, reacts according to what we believe individually and collectively, to what you think and believe constitutes your life as it is today. Change your beliefs and thinking and you change your world. Universal law deals with the law of attraction, what you believe and what you know is what you attract to yourself.

Change Must Come or the Only Thing Permanent is Change

The dysfunction of human society is the result of our thinking. We must end our actions, which are reactions drawn from the collective unconscious beliefs. These no longer apply. Like an outdated map, this lack of connection is an old pattern that is no longer applicable. Collectively, our thinking either resides in past or an illusive future. We have evolved in many ways, but our primitive inheritance remains. As the primitive man lived with fear for survival, so do we. Still mimicking our ancestors' ways, we are afraid of each other, instead of caring for each other.

Whatever we fight or flee, fear continues to plague us until we change and embrace love. (What we resist persists.) All we hear is of war: war against drugs, terrorism, cancer, crime, poverty, this, or that. There are wars on almost everything because we fear everything. It makes sense fear, punishment, and war don't resolve anything. Don't take my word, just check the numbers of people in the U.S. prison system and you will see the numbers have gone from thirty thousand to two point one million in the last 10 years.

Wars have forced man to invent weapons to fight everything including drugs to fight new diseases, which are invented or created by the drug companies and the media. Look at the commercials on TV and you will notice a new disease has been discovered each year. This is evidence the war is in the mind-set, which creates the enemy. Once we defeat this enemy, the affect is that a new

Chapter Five — All Happens As It Should

and stronger enemy emerges in the aftermath.

The question is: why and what are our fears? The answer is: they are the effects of an enemy we have created in the first place. What we don't understand, we fear. We fear what is different from us because we don't understand what it is. The old meaning for the word fear was to understand. What we fear we bring upon ourselves. This means what we know or understand, or don't understand in many cases we bring to us in consciousness.

There is nothing to fear because we are all passengers on the same space ship called Earth. One race and species, humanity, we are all of one source. Of course, there are many, languages, cultures, and beliefs, but one source and this is composed of infinite variety. Just as there are many stars and planets in the Universe, we are all the parts that make up the one.

With all our differences, our interests are the same. When Abraham Maslow wrote his hierarchy of needs he looked at humanity as a whole. Our desire to survive is followed by the need to be accepted and loved, to know, and finally to have self-realization where we understand our true-identity. I would add life in general needs to communicate so its cooperation can happen. Even the birds tell my little dog it must cooperate for life to continue.

Reflective Consciousness

Our reactions against the things we despise in each other are the things that are also in us. Memories of events, beliefs, dogmas, experiences, are the content that is a part of our thought. As consciousness aware of itself as consciousness, we are always looking into the mirror of our own unconscious mind. Understanding memories gives humanity a sense of continuity. Our very nature is eternal and infinitely present at all times. To even say consciousness does not exist is to prove its existence. We contain the whole history, the whole universe within our consciousness. Our life is a looking glass. We are always reflecting in our reactions and inactions what our mind is thinking. We carry the fear and love within. When we react to another, we are reacting to our personal consciousness.

Being in the Now

Our mind explodes everyday with pulsing of billions of neurons. These miniature threads of consciousness are looped together in our mind to make sense of our experiences. What we know is we are capable of living in multiple dimensions, universes, and worlds at any one moment.

Stop for a moment, take a deep breath slowly

CHAPTER FIVE   ALL HAPPENS AS IT SHOULD

and let it out. Focus on the breath for this moment only. In this one moment, all life is exactly as it should be. You are total, whole, and complete. By staying present you refuse to live in the past and fantasize about the future. Your consciousness has the ability at this one moment to know you are connected to all life, By nature we are existential in our being. When Christ said "only as a little child may you enter the house of the Father," he was speaking of this existential nature. The miracle and gift of life is knowing; in the connection we find our purpose of existence and the meaning to our life. We are fulfilled.

NOW IS THE REALITY THAT WE MUST AWAKE TO.

Being present is the only way to experience life. Past and future are illusions. Life requires your presence. Only with our eyes wide open do we find what we long to know and have in our life. With eyes wide open humanity can learn to feed the hungry, care for the ill, and embrace all that come to be.

The new age we approach demands we understand principle and cosmic spiritual law. Humanity continues to believe that 2+2=5. It sins (misses the mark). Once we understand that principle is 2+2=4 it all becomes extraordinarily simple. None of us have more God or love than another. None of us have more Truth or consciousness. It is as Einstein said, everything is evenly present for us all.

BRAVE NEW WORLD

Each child will be taught the principles of love. In this all healing will take place. Children will be safe to walk the streets in wonderment, fill their growing bodies with clean water and healthy food. With their eyes open they will explore the beautiful world that is present for them.

It is up to us, to make this happen. None of us can sit idly by letting our brothers do the work. Our work is to clarify our consciousness and embrace the world as a spiritual and sacred place. When we become intimate with our being as a creation of the Creator, we experience the sacred thoughts of the Creator source, God thoughts, the Truth in its entire splendor. Once we create this place in our consciousness, we are forever free. Freedom, health, and love all begin in our mind. The brave new world is the world of understanding our existential existence with all life as sacred beings.

WHERE TO START

We start with ourselves, freeing ourselves from the slavery of the past, then our families, and schools. We teach our children more than reading and writing, we teach them about absolute love and being one in the community of humanity. Next, we take it to our leaders demanding leadership is compassionate, strong, and able to help all of humanity, not merely special interests.

All of the masters have written and spoken about this work. This is our work. This is the path to free your self from the slavery of false beliefs. Like Moses, Gandhi, Buddha, and millions of others this is your opportunity, my opportunity, to heal the world and ourselves.

From our thoughts, we create form and all of our experiences, including our world and every situation. All are a manifestation of an inner, invisible Intelligence. This collective human consciousness is the force behind the events and the life on our planet. If we are to change the kind of life on earth, we must transform the state of human consciousness. To accomplish this you must, first transform your consciousness. As the old consciousness dissolves, a new life emerges, and thus, a new planet.

The physical or mechanical mind is not the mind that creates. True creation must come from the Spirit. Creation does not make mistakes. We must allow the Spirit to create for us, by our ability to think with our higher mind. We have access to this mind through our spiritual nature.

Take a deep breath and let go of the past, exhale

it out, inhale the pure light of absolute love. Allow the splendor you are to shine forth giving you the light and courage upon the path we must all walk. Join with me, grasp my hand. As one of us goes so do we all.

Do you hear it? A billion stars are singing. A billion suns laughing for the joy of it all! Do you hear it? Do you hear the moons of eternity calling us to join the Universe? Take my hand and we will make it.

Chapter Five — All Happens As It Should

Where Can I Start?
Notes

"I believe in the power of intention to change the landscape of our society - and it is my intention to live an authentic life of compassion and integrity and action."

~Zachary Quinto

Chapter 6

Embracing Our Differences

The intention of governments and their function was to provide a group or community with protective programs and structure, which benefits groups, and guides those in need. It was never about building businesses or excluding others.

The Road To Hell Is Paved In Good Intentions

Intentions of governments are many, but rarely do they deliver upon the expectations. They are supposed to provide the resources and tools to benefit all, the whole of the citizenry. Government functions according to the leaders, and leaders are elected by the citizens in a democracy. It does no good to point fingers and blame each other. Our collective consciousness is at work.

At the dawn of Ayn Rand's philosophy in the early 1960's in the United States and around the world, a new leadership emerged, one whose directive was to get people what they wanted. A leader was defined as a person who could best procure what the followers wanted. Along with this new leadership, unprecedented greed and power emerged in the world.

By the end of the 60's, consciousness was exploding all around us with new awareness. As citizens, we no longer accepted the idea war was an answer. Old ideals were being thrown to the wind. Along came the 80's and Ronald Regan became the symbol of leadership around the globe. It was the "Me" generation. And leadership was determined to allow greed to grow. At this time, the world started to be connected in a way that had never happened before. The Internet was born. This was to change the whole paradigm of our world.

With the Internet, came a new kind of transparency. The savagery and slavery of most of the world was revealed. In real time, we saw we weren't surviving. Our world was dying of over population. World leaders were choking us. Along with greed and manipulation came an awakening. Now we are able to see what is happening in real time. Our eyes are no longer shut. Now we must face our leadership and our own collective unconsciousness.

As long as leaders got us what we wanted, we

CHAPTER SIX   EMBRACING OUR DIFFERENCES

closed our eyes to the fear mongering and lies. But now we understand we need a new kind of leader. We don't need to recapture old ethics and ideals; we need to create new kinds of compassionate leaders. Leaders who don't desire power, but see leadership as a kind of servitude; leaders who don't think they are God-like, but understand the spiritual needs of those they serve.

The old style of leadership equated truth with their beliefs. They went so far as preserving their beliefs at all costs. Even now, they will even justify these illusive truths by killing non-believers. It shows we are dealing with ignorance, blindsided by the fear of our differences, instead of embracing them. We can't fix our world until we are willing to embrace and share our differences.

In the end there is only one truth and you are IT. You are the truth, it is in you, but if you look for it elsewhere, you will not find it. Jesus said: "I am the way and the truth and the light." Though it points to the truth but it's not IT. There is only one absolute truth where all others have their source. Actions can either reflect truth or illusion.

Will you join with me in becoming a new kind of leader? Enter into our brave world as Truth. It is you, and only you who can make these changes. We can do this together.

"I refuse to accept the view that mankind is so tragically bound to the starless midnight of racism and war; that the bright daybreak of peace and brotherhood can never become a reality... I believe unarmed truth and unconditional love will have the final word."

~Martin Luther King, Jr.

Chapter 7

Reality As We Know It

The basis of our reality is not found in worldly influences; it is based in spirituality and in our essence. There are over six billion people on earth and we are all connected. We are all woven into the mesh of the Universal fabric. Just as the planets, the stars, and galaxies, we are in the web of the psychic and magnetic field. This is the womb of creative energy from whence all things come. We use this medium to create and manifest our life experiences.

Science has proven that the Universe and everything in it will return to its original state of nothingness or formlessness. Just as the Universe has expanded since the Big Bang, it will shrink back to nothingness; its origin, which is pure energy. It will go through the same cycle over again. Nothing in the Universe ever dies. The Universe does not waste, everything is simply transformed.

Our lives and bodies go through the same cycle: beginning, the explosion of creative life force until the time of vanishing and transition, to nothingness, thus becoming energy, its origin. These transitions include everything: government, beliefs, and our consciousness. All falls into the same cycle of temporal existence.

A new era of consciousness is arising, one transcending thought and physical limitations. Humanity is awakening to the dimensions that exist within ourselves, infinitely vaster than we thought. We refer to the old and the past parts of human existence to create our lives, but these are constructed out of old and failing patterns. These habits of identification with human-inheritance-memory are still unchanged. We still create the same evil because we can't function without our identification with the old. Until we learn that we are beyond thought, beyond the world of things, we can be at our purest state of being, and identify with our original self, we will always fall prey to the distractions.

When you no longer need to think of who you are and rise to the space of being—this is when enlightenment takes place. It is at this place where limitations are no longer an issue. It is here that everything is known and there is nothing to know beyond that.

Chapter Seven — Reality As We Know It

What Will It Take?

What will it take humanity to transform, come together as one, and make the world the place it was meant to be? It takes you and me, willing to change our consciousness, willing to step over the chasm of fear and belief. Looking over the chasm, we hear the screams in our head, we feel the chaos and quiver in our fear of falling. Courage is not easy to come by. Your desire to change and open up to IT, your true nature, must be so great that it overrides your fears. Sometimes it takes a catastrophe, or a great sadness before we can say, "What do I have to lose?" Sometimes, it takes our whole life to get to the point where we have the courage to step over that great chasm, to where we can leap into sanity embracing our true identity.

Creation

We have this need, to reach beyond our present situation, to something outside of ourselves. We reach to break free of the limiting bonds set on us by our beliefs, and the experiences that have come to reinforce those beliefs. We seek to understand the beginning of our consciousness, our life, and to understand the path we will follow upon death. Life without an understanding of creation seems void of meaning and connection. Death without everlasting life is unspeakable for most of us.

A True State of Aloneness

Just as it is hard to fully conceive of the infinite, so is it hard to understand the finality or finiteness of life. Infinity is a state of being rather than an intellectual concept that must be understood. To embrace an experience of infinity we must step outside our intellectual and emotional life, allowing our beliefs and experiences to be put aside. As you shed the intellectual understanding of infinity, letting go of time and space as relative factors and embracing them as an experience, you are left with nothing, no reference points, not a sequences of events, no familiarity.

At that point, you become beingness experiencing beingness. We are finally and totally alone without others or mind or spirit. Just to be is neither intellectual nor emotional. Just being is a sensual experience where all things become nonthings, where all time that was IS, and all that will be IS. Nothing exists outside of this one sensual state of being. This is an act of pure creation. It is without the infinite or the finite. This is a state, if we are lucky, we experience at least once in our life. It holds all answers therefore no answer. To understand this state, we must understand how our intellect comes to believe and the experiences of life and death.

Chapter Seven — Reality As We Know It

Unity

Lessons present themselves when you are ready to receive them. It does not matter what you do, what matters is in every situation there is a purpose. Your purpose is found by acceptance of what is. Meaning life can only be lived in the now. God can only be found in the now moment.

How you live in the present lays the groundwork for the future. What you choose to think, say, and do is only possible in the present. Presence allows you to listen to others and be where they are. This openness allows learning and self-growth. There are differences, but the differences are the components of the whole and the many parts that make up One.

As the Universe is filled with infinite diversity, we humans are an example of the infinite manifestations with all our differences. As the Universe operates in harmony with all the diversity, so can humans with all our cultures, views, and beliefs, because in the end we are all of one; part of the same life, same Universe, of One source, all of us have our origin in One.

No one escapes birth or death. For a moment, our very fears can unite us. It is our own courage we must stand and face as humanity. Courage will pull us into sanity. The leap into sanity is one of unity. We find we are part of a great chorus of humanity. Our infinite manifestations shine forth the beauty of our differences. Separation and exclusion are a kind of insanity.

Can we pause for a moment and find a way to come together? Now? I suggest we embrace our differences as a way to teach each other. It is the differences between us and other, all of them, that make up our own missing parts. It is the differences between individuals, which complete us. We have gone too long inflicting pain and suffering on each other. By far, the greatest reason humans inflict pain and suffering on each other is not the work of criminals, but the work of normal, responsible individuals who are ego driven.

Normal is the insanity that plagues our world. The truth is, it is fear which triggers the reactive impulse to violence. We fear what we don't understand in one another. These unknown phenomena are exactly what we are missing, and need to have, in order to be complete.

Come hold my hand, leap with me into sanity. If we do it together we will have the courage to live as our true being. Please, take my hand.

CHAPTER SEVEN   REALITY AS WE KNOW IT

What Do I Need To Do
Notes

"A house must be built on solid foundations if it is to last. The same principle applies to man, otherwise he too will sink back into the soft ground and becomes swallowed up by the world of illusion."

~Sai Baba

Chapter 8

The Opium of Illusion

Illusion is perhaps one of the hardest concepts for spiritual students to grasp. Our senses tell us the world is solid and our mind believes what is being reported to us. Illusion, the dream state, is like an opium to our ego. We get hooked on it all at a very young age. We must give up our addiction to the dream, the illusion, that there is something separating us.

Science tells us it is not the flower we see but rather the light reflecting off of the flower. Our unconscious mind then can identify the flower according to the reflective light. If our experiences and beliefs tell us the flower is poison, we will recoil from it. What we know if the flower is poison to us it will react as poison in our body. But to another who does not have our belief it will be much different. American Natives will eat scorpions saying they give them strength. If you or I were to eat one we would become ill. It is through our beliefs that life appears as it does to us.

What appears before us is but a dream. There is no physical reality. Much of what we must grasp, if we are to change our current path, cannot be seen. We must rely on our ability to be observant to recognize the patterns of false beliefs. These false beliefs keep us from recognizing the Truth, reality.

Science tells us most of the volume of an atom is empty space, just like the Universe. There is no outside of an atom. All life is an ebbing and flowing of energy. We are full of holes and spaces. In the eyes of science there is nothing solid or steady about us. Life appears as it is because the collective unconscious of humanity. There is no principle that says red is red; it is an agreed upon name. No matter what language you speak the concept of red remains red because of the unconscious data we have collected through billions of years. Red is an agreed upon definition in the collective unconscious mind.

Governments, rules, and religions are types of collective illusion. We have decided they are the way they are as a collective. Don't be duped into believing these aren't real, or getting rid of these illusions is easy. It is in every cell of our being through billions of years these things are as they appear to us.

Chapter Eight — The Opium of Illusion

Humanity creates gods. This starts as a young babe at the feet of our parents. We look at them as the giver and taker of life (a good definition of what we call a God). And thus begins our creation of gods in our life. Our gods can be power, money, beauty, or anything you want them to be. How can we be intimate with the concept of God if we give it such a temporal definition in our lives?

We sit together in this great theater of life projecting onto the screen our current movie. It is as simple as deciding we no longer want this movie. Change the movie, get rid of the illusion and you get rid of the pain and poverty in the world.

There isn't an old wise man with a long flowing beard that will come to save us. Whatever you worship or may think is the one image of God, let me tell you: IT'S NOT IT! The human mind cannot grasp it. Religions (including secular religions like nationalities) are concepts we have created. Through these concepts, we have elected leaders to lead and govern us. What we have created are prisons in our minds.

Rules and governments are made because we have not yet broken free from the prison of our egos. Our mental prison is a plane of dysfunction, which still operates in a primitive mode of survival. We have not evolved from our primitive ways. By going beyond the illusion, we will break through the fear and see we are the ego that must be overcome. The ego hides behind the need to be human and wants to deceive us so we will identify with it.

This book may be controversial to some, but it will have an impact on you. I hope it will make you think. Whatever you do, say and think belongs to you. It comes from you, so it's yours. It will come back to you.

The courage to be takes us out of the illusion of ordinary into an extraordinary state of existence. Our lives become one of embracing individuality and yet understanding the core of all life is of one idea no matter what it is called. Those with courage of being don't have to spout their passion, they live it. They are willing to stand up in the face of adversity for what is Truth and right for all. Those with the courage to protect children from the rhetoric of fear and the opium of delusion. Individuality becomes a source of pride and celebration. Freedom for all is the major premise of their governing law.

The courage to be is more than accepting Truth. It is about freeing our minds from the captivity of the delusion of freedom and ego. Will you please join me in the climb up the mountain? We will find freedom from the slavery of this make believe world in the true nature of reality. The freedom to love fully, laugh often, and feel deeply. The climb is easier if we do it together.

Notes on Illusions

"Shallow men believe in luck. Strong men believe in cause and effect."

~Ralph Waldo Emerson

Chapter 9

You Are The Paradox

Every person is a person. Every person, including me and you, is part of the whole. Regardless where you are from, what culture and belief system, you are the cause and life is the effect.

The Law of Cause and Effect

The practice of mindfulness in all areas of life produces pragmatic understanding of how our mind works. In our observation of our thoughts we can learn how our body, our whole being, follows the command of the thoughts. If we stand and breathe and the thought comes to us to sit we will sit. If the thought is to move forward, our body will respond with the urge and will to move forward. The body and being will respond to all thought no matter what it is. This is important to understand for all our life responds to our thoughts.

Our actions and the response of the world around us are linked, not as two actions, but as one consciousness. The going and the doing cannot be separated from the thought. The body and mind are one concept, not separate. Cause and effect are one idea. In examining the paradox of this idea we come to a new understanding of the use of mindfulness in our everyday life. This is to say that every action we take will have a bearing on how our life unfolds to us, for we are the causer and as well as the recipient of the effect.

The understanding of all life meets at this point where we see we are the causer and the recipient of the effect. Paradoxes play an important role in life, for they bring cause and effect to the same point of understanding. Within each paradox is an understanding about the nature of life that will free us from a limiting belief about our self, family, work, and our culture.

The solutions to all life's problems can be found at the paradox point, where the finite thought and the idea of infinity meet. If you don't understand what I am writing, don't worry, these are ideas that we can only grasp for a few minutes at time. Monks and priests spend lifetimes contemplating them. What you need to know is anytime you find a conflict of thought you are dealing with cause and effect. You are dealing with the problem and solution in the same point. When we look into the paradox point, we do not understand the head and tails of a coin as separate entities. They do not stand alone, but rather what appears at first glance to be separate is one idea much greater than the individual parts.

To gain insight into the process of our life and obtaining our goals, we must become aware that each of our thoughts, no matter how lowly or seemingly insignificant, has an effect on our life. Thus, thoughts are the causer. The understanding of cause and effect in our thinking is a lifelong process.

Major causes of disruption in our lives are our intolerances and clinging to beliefs that no longer work. If we believe as we did as a child our adult life will be confusing and painful. How can we function using the child's ideas of life? Our ego keeps us from seeing how our life plays out and where our responsibility lies. The ego would have us believe others are at fault and our thinking is fine.

Any perception that we are separate from the causer, which is from our consciousness expressing as our world, is an illusion. Our perceptions are built upon beliefs. It is like having a pair of colored glasses on all the time: eventually you get used to the distortion of color and ignore the illusion. The fantasy still exists you just end up ignoring it.

We have been taught things happen to us, so it has become a belief and perception in our lives. Like the colored glasses, we have grown accustomed to the illusion, the dream, and have come to think this is reality; the causer is outside of our consciousness. If we place the causer outside of our self, we have become separate from the creative powers and the reality of our world. Like all hostages (for we are all hostages to our beliefs and illusions), we side with the enemy. The enemy is the ego, the belief and perception that we are aren't the causer and have been separated from our core being.

The ego terrorizes us. It tells us, if we let go of our colored glasses we will not be able to see, to cope with life. We allow ourselves to be held as a hostage to the fears we have grown in ourselves from childish beliefs and understanding. The only way to face down the terrorizing bully of this ego is to call its bluff. Take the colored glasses off look clearly at the beauty your life can be.

We perceive according to beliefs. A hypnotist will tell an audience member the temperature of the room is very hot. This implanted belief causes the person to start to sweat. The temperature might in fact be cool, but the perception of heat is there and the body reacts to this. This happens to us each day. We believe something and it becomes a reality to us. We believe something is

Chapter Nine — You Are The Paradox

harmful, or we believe something is good, and we react accordingly. Our thoughts and beliefs direct our every movement.

It is impossible to have dominion over your life if you are separated from what is producing life as you know it. The broader the picture in your reality, the more options you have. As long as you are separate from the concept your thoughts, beliefs, and perceptions are forming your life, you have no way of changing your life. The more you get rid of limiting beliefs taught to you by your family, schools, and culture, the freer you are to direct your life in a fulfilling manner. The idea anyone other than yourself is the causer in your life is illusionary.

Gaining dominion over your life does not mean you will be wealthy or famous. It does mean you have a way of looking at life that is fulfilling and exciting. It means the inner turmoil can be lessened, that painful situations will be understood, and the patterns, which are disruptive causers in your life, are changed. In the end, it is a journey of intentional consciousness. Like waking from deep slumber, our world takes on a fresh, exciting aspect. We are the creator as consciousness. You will find the purpose of your being.

How This Works

We are directing the events of our world and, at the same time, being programmed by the messages that come back to us. It shows in the news we watch. Our thoughts are constantly attracting the situations of our awareness and experiences.

The media is constantly innundating our minds to capture our attention. We are in a state of captivity. To keep us there, to feed our ennui, they create more news, affecting our lives one-way or another. The news we watch never contains the information that will induce the connectivity we so desperately need in order to bridge and bond us. The mother in a refugee camp somewhere in Africa or Cambodia is defying impossible odds in order to feed her children and keep them safe: we never get the news of her story. She will never be able to tell the world about the execution of a worthless war conducted by some evil, low-life hoodlums.

Where We Start

We start by removing the colored glasses we have been wearing. We look at ourselves clearly in the mirror. As we begin to see, we accept our responsibility and part in the world that we live in. Welcome the paradox and know that before the problem can exist the answer must be. An authentic life awaits you.

Chapter Nine — You Are The Paradox

Join me as we step through the circle of fire, where our false attitudes and beliefs are shed for our authentic self. And like the phoenix, we will rise from the ashes together as one world united. Join me the answer awaits us.

My Paradox

"Had we not loved ourselves at all, we could never have been obliged to love anything. So that self-love is the basis of all love."

~Thomas Traherne

Chapter 10

Self-Love

Let Your Heart And Spirit Lead

Self-love is the single most powerful tool we have, but so few of us ever master and most only ever know and experience a glimpse of it. If you can only exercise one muscle on the road of life, it must be self-love. You cannot honestly, unconsciously or consciously give love if you cannot love yourself.

When all is said and done, what is it we are looking and craving for? It is love, everything we do, say, and think is motivated by the desire to love and be loved. We seek our great fortunes, beautiful bodies, and all manner of status symbols, being fooled into thinking if we have more things, we will be more lovable. I guarantee you, if you think you will be happier once you hit the lottery, you are gravely mistaken.

The Ultimate Healer

All creation is an act of love. Love is more than an emotion it is a movement in consciousness. As a flow of energy and grace, it moves from in to out. Love's movement is powerful: so potent it can heal a physical wound, emotional injustice, and bring life into being. That which is created in consciousness, in an act of love, is forever and eternal in nature.

For life to thrive it must be loved. As consciousness, we are always creating love and standing in love. It is impossible to be conscious without love. Love is an act of acceptance and giving. To want to be loved is as natural as breathing. A simple act of love can change the very chemistry of our body. A plant that is loved thrives, as do children, and all other life. The very act of living is an act of love.

Once an act of conscious love is committed and it can never undone. It may change form, unfold, and become something new, but conscious love can never be over. Once you have loved, no matter whom you have loved or what has been done to your love; love is forever. Our consciousness changes, unfolds we rediscover our true being when we give love and accept love. There is only one cure for the world and what ails it. And this is love, an unconditional acceptance of all being as consciousness created in an act of love. The only path to healing of any sort is the path of love.

Chapter Ten — Self-Love

Absolute love is, in spiritual and ontological terms, the flow of God-energy through us all. Unconditional love sees God or Truth in all there is. It does not judge the broken arm or the dirty face, the differently colored skin, nor language, nor perception as an error, but rather sees these states as Truth manifesting in infinite variety. When we fall in love, we touch the spirit and consciousness of the other. It is impossible to love the physical body. The physical body is only a representation in this process of the spirit. It comes to represent to us the other's spirit. We love the spirit of each other. Our spirits are of the same source. Unless we can practice self-love, how can we embrace the one creative source?

Absolute love is responsive to needs of consciousness. Absolute love is receptive to our need to explore and to know the nature of our existence through our sensuality. It does not judge nor does it itself seem to need anything. Unconditional love flows from a place of absolute being where we accept ourselves as spirit, as consciousness aware of itself as consciousness. The flow of this energy is the same flow as a meditation or a prayer, meaning it flows from in to out and back as the motion of a wave.

Love Without Expectations

While absolute love always exists we are often not aware of it. There are many states of love and consciousness about love. There is a need within us to define, outline, and give reason. This need leads us to place conditions on our love. Often, the love we experience is filled with conditions. We love friends because of shared experiences, interests, support, and communication. These become the conditions of the love. When we have conditions on love, it is not absolute. The test of absolute love is to see if the love remains once the conditions have been removed.

Placing expectations on relationships and circumstances places conditions in such a manner absolute love is blocked. To have intentional consciousness about absolute love we must remove our expectations and allow the love to flow. By allowing love to flow without conditions you free yourself and relationships from limitations from the conditions that keep you from fully experiencing the power, healing, and experience of love.

Unconditional love is not just heart-centered love, it is the very core of the Universe, the cohesive force we experience as consciousness. As an aspect of consciousness, it takes practice to live in a state of unconditional love. To love without expectations of behavior or relationship is to accept the beingness, the existence of all life.

Love without expectations, unconditional love is not personal. It is an acceptance total, complete, and perfect of all life. It does not come and go, waiver, or grow weak …it just is.

Chapter Ten — Self-Love

Seeking Love

Seeking love is as natural as breathing. Our first cries are to our mother, our progenitor arms stretch out saying take, love, and know me. We seek to have this chrysalis, this shell we call body penetrated and known. We seek to be accepted as we are. In this seeking, we search for our beloved. At first, we think we need another being to find our soul mate. We look for the perfect partner who will know us to the core and accept all of us the good, bad, and what we create. The answers we seek about our aloneness aren't found in the arms of another human being, but rather in our consciousness. Acceptance and love we want begins with awareness of our self and self-love.

Our beloved is our I AM, it is the higher consciousness. The blind leap of faith in love is simply taking the plunge over the edge of the chasm of insanity into the arms of the beloved, which is higher consciousness.

You can only experience what is in your consciousness. What is outside of your consciousness has no existence to you. Just as 2+2=4 has no knowledge of 2+2=5. 2+2=5 is outside of the realm of mathematical principle and has no existence in math.

To know that love exists means that it is within your consciousness. Love is the cohesive force within your consciousness, just as the Creator is within your consciousness. What has existence cannot be lost. Consciousness does not hide and neither can love. The experience of love is always with you. You are always standing in love. Every act is an act of love. You have to but open your eyes for it to be revealed to you. Consciousness has no existence outside of love. Love is the illumination of consciousness. It is the cohesive force, which gives us purpose, and destiny. In love, we are immortal.

The Real Winners

The media will have you believe big winners in the arena of fame, fortune, and beauty are happier than you. This is a complete fallacy. Unless you can look inside of yourself and love who you are, absolutely nothing of this material world will make a dent in your pain and suffering.

There is a much larger picture you should be aware of that is not often perceived. We are part of the same universal source. We long to be with one another and exchange of our inner gifts. It is ignorance which keeps us apart and from knowing why we are on this planet in the first place.

Chapter Ten — Self-Love

We come here for a brief moment with an opportunity to burn a mark on this earth, but we are told that is by becoming rich and famous. How absurd. Then why is that the most influential people to ever to walk the earth where paupers, such as Jesus, Gandhi, Mother Teresa, and Buddha These where all people who owned nothing more than the clothes on their back, yet these are still the ones whose example the whole world follows. There are things that can only be achieved in the realm of spirituality.

The purpose of our bodies is to house our spirits. The single purpose of our spirit is to communicate love. Expressions of love between human beings are the key that can make a difference in this life. It serves us no purpose to try to fix others or situations before we heal jour own suffering and feelings of separation. We must first embrace the self, and find absolute love. Love is key. Love your body, love your soul, love yourself totality.

Every act of love is beautiful, and full of grace and must include the self. There is nothing to love outside of the self, for the world is a reflection of the self.

You are the home you live in, so take care of your home, by keeping it clean, and by planting beautiful flowers. Love yourself. It will bring out the best in you. When you have accepted your true self, your beingness, and you will know you are a vessel of absolute love. Your spiritual being will be nourished beyond all expectations. Each day becomes a day of beauty, a day where your consciousness grows and unfolds to miracles yet to be known.

The person who can embrace their existence through loving themselves is automatically charismatic. Others are attracted to you; they want to know what you have. You become a symbol of the beloved for all. Once you have embraced the self with love, others can't help but love you. A person that does not love him/herself will not love another. What you think is love of another is an unfulfilled desire. Only loving yourself can you have a loving relationship with another person.

Return to the Heart

It is impossible for us not to be love. All of life is created from a state of love. No matter what you were told about your conception and birth, you are a child of love. Life does not exist without love. Love bridges all races, all people, all life to find an expression. Nothing can harm or stop love. In simpler words, return to a state of being known as heart felt reality.

Teach your children and grandchildren about love. Teach them the world was created out of love and is love. Teach them love is kind and gen-

Chapter Ten — Self-Love

tle and embraces all of humanity. You can give no greater gift than the knowledge and practice of love as a heart reality. The more love a child is given, the more self-love they develop. The embracing of love makes it easier for them on their personal journey. Each experience in their life will bring them closer to Truth, and being embraced by the nature of reality.

Love is not some make believe ideal. It is not something the weak practice. To love and be loved takes a strong individual. Someone who is willing to let go of their, ego for a greater good. You are a creature of love having a human experience. If you were to ask me why we exist on this globe at this time, I will tell you we are here to experience and know we are love. Love is why we came here, love is who we are… love is what we do.

Take my hand as we walk this path of beauty, grace, and eternal love. A million sunrises sing our songs. A billion stars light our path through eternity as beings of love. Take my hand and know you are not alone but are joining the great chorus of love called humanity.

"It is the prayer of my innermost being to realize my supreme identity in the liberated play of consciousness, the Vast Expanse. Now is the moment, here is the place of Liberation."

~Alex Grey

Chapter 11

Identity

The immediate question upon the birth of a baby is 'is it a boy or girl?' This one incident starts building the identity of the individual. Our parents introduce us to others as their son or daughter and we learn our surname. Eventually we become the artist, the worker, the husband or wife, the parent, plus a thousand other roles help create who we think we are.

We think our individuality, our self, is based in all of these roles we have taken on. We loose a job and we are devastated because we have lost the identity the work gave us. A wife looses a husband suddenly and finds she is unable to know who she is now. All of this confusion and pain because we have placed our identity in temporal concepts.

The essence of our being is not limited to our work, relationship, or place of birth. Identity has nothing to do with race, religion, and our surname. We misunderstand who we are. If we create our identity based on the roles we have in life, then we become unconscious of our inner essence. Our inner purpose becomes buried under the rules, status, and concepts that are manmade.

When we say and believe this is who we are; be aware this is how we perceive ourselves and how others see us. But this is not It.

Our true-identity is one of consciousness. As consciousness aware of consciousness, we are unlimited in who and what we are. We are no longer bound by false identities of person and place. Our heritage is not one given to use by our parents but the heritage of unlimited consciousness manifesting in infinite variety.

Do we have bodies? Yes, but this is not our real identity. Our bodies are a human experience. We are spiritual beings having a human experience. One of the disciples asked Jesus if he should pay taxes and Jesus said, "Render unto Caesar that which is Caesar's and give to God that which is the father's. For I am in this world but not of it."

Every prophet, sage, and powerful person has known this, the truth of their real identity: they are not of this world. This means you are not of a physical essence, but of light, spirit.

Chapter Eleven — Identity

All you have to do is look at public induced life styles of movie stars and see what a false identity can do to an individual. The stars we watch are often deep into alcohol, drugs and despair. They are either hiding or trying to figure out who they are. We want to be known, we want to know who we really are. This is a kind of yearning.

The Yearning

There is in all of us a longing, a desire to be known. We seek to be known, not in a famous way, but to be known for who we truly are, as essence. This yearning to be known is about being accepted. The need for acceptance is overwhelming in many of us. Perhaps as many psychologists tell us it begins at the separation of birth. For whatever the reason this need, this yearning to be known, is a driving force that forms many relationships and a large amount of our actions.

What is it exactly we want another to know about us? What is this yearning this hunger , which so motivates us into relationships and actions?

Perhaps the easy answer is we want our spirit known. The tough answer is we want to know our self, to penetrate our outer fantasy and illusions to find our own spirit of being. We must accept our own being. Our acceptance of self can't happen in a fantasy existence of a past and future. It can only happen in the NOW moment. In this moment, the only moment we have we must accept our I AM I state of being if we are to be known. To know who we are--what we are--this is the first step in finding our Cosmic Intent. To find our Cosmic Intent, we must penetrate our own fantasy and delusions to the core of our being I AM I.

This great and extraordinary being we are cannot be known if it is covered by false identities, and the make believe world we have built. You are not the fantasy: you are the world. Young children know they are not of this world. They know that their parents are caregivers not their true father and mother. Ask any mother or father who has adopted a child and they will tell you: blood identity had nothing to do with their love for a child.

Our consciousness is not a static state. Our being or existence continues to grow, accumulating ideas and experiences. Layer after layer of fantasy about whom we are, what we are, and where we are going in our life are filed into our unconscious.

We are constantly pricked by the voice of the ego filling our head with chatter, keeping us asleep, and hidden from our self. This constant head chatter is mesmerizing. We become fascinated by the sound of our own thoughts. We drown out any possibility of hearing the quietness of being.

The law of nature is a movement from in to out, unfolding, and revelation. Staying in fantasy and delusion states keeps us static. We rot, grow old, tired, and stop living when we are inert. Each of us holds a piece of life, which contains all the purpose, meaning and infinity of being. This consciousness is not dormant. This consciousness is constantly growing and unfolding, bringing meaning and purpose to the one moment we have.

Like the softness of dawn, this consciousness plays upon our being. We have only to stop, get quiet, and let it reveal its beauty to us. When we stay in the NOW we allow our consciousness to reveal to us the purpose of our being, our cosmic intent, our reason for existence. The moment of revelation of purpose is a moment of ecstatic pleasure. This pleasure is for us all to experience.

The only thing you need to do is become present in the NOW, quiet the ego-mind, and allow the dawn to unfold in your life. Let go of the illusion and fantasy you think you are and embrace the real you.

Awaken

The purpose of our being never goes away. It is impossible to hide from it, for it follows you like a beloved everywhere you go. The verve to explore the purpose of our being is strong within us. We can try to hide behind the ego mind, behind our veils of delusion, but it finds us. Sometimes it finds us in our nightly dreams, sometimes it comes through our delusional states, and we see it very clearly. Like being awakened early in the morning, we turn our back to the light and pull the cover over our head.

Compulsively returning to the past and running toward the future helps us hide from our purpose and true-identity. And as long as we hide, we remain asleep. Only when we stay present and in this moment accepting what is, can we know our purpose of being, our Cosmic Intent. When we stay present and accept this moment, accept that which is so, the veils of illusion are lifted from our eyes, and like dawn, the light awakens us. We are similar to small children being protected by those who have awakened to their purpose of being and true-identity, and because of this we are never awakened with our eyes open to the sun.

You will not be burned by the light of the dawn. The joy of finding your self will never leave you. Awaken with me to the Joy awaiting us.

Chapter Eleven — Identity

Who Am I
Notes

"Love is the great miracle cure. Loving ourselves works miracles in our lives."

~Louise L. Hay

Chapter 12

The Miracle of Surrender, Healing

One my many experiences in life was being a bodyguard for celebrities. One of these celebrities was Lindsay Lohan. I was her bodyguard during the making of the movie *Herbie*. I witnessed many things during that period, but the most important, which had the most impact in my experience, was of young beautiful girl with so much potential, being pushed into an artificial life, with no love or soul. Without having a chance to experience the most important time of her life as a teenager, with kids of her age, she was missing out on her childhood. Working most of the time from sunrise to sunset, she was surrounded by producers and workers 3 times her age. Her life and identity was written on the scripts of the movies in which she acted. I had a glimpse of the beautiful human being, who just wanted to be loved for her true self. I tried to help and guide her, but when one of the parents saw my help might jeopardize their earnings they made sure I was no longer needed it. The problem with Lindsay, still a teenager, was she did not have a mother and father present. Whatever trials she caused were to get their attention. She was desperately looking for love and support. Well, she found the replacement, in drugs and alcohol.

There are many illnesses in the world today. Illusion or not, they exist, and we succumb to them out of our ignorance. It is hard to get past the idea we are a physical body, and as long as we are a physical body, we are going to become ill. Mentally or physically we will succumb to them. Mental health experts rarely have an answer. Allopathic and Psychiatric physicians thrive on handing out little pills. Have a quandary, take a pill. This is not to put down any medical system, but rather look at what we have allowed to happen. We can't say Truth is all there is, God is all there and then this group over here is not God or Truth. All medical practices, allopathy and alternative, deal with the symptoms rather than the causer. For a real healing, to take place we must deal with the causer.

To truly heal we must surrender to higher power and let the will of God have its way with us. The real healing comes when we let go of our ego mind and begin to see we do have choices.

Chapter Twelve — Healing

The Anatomy of a Miracle

For any miracle or healing to occur we must transcend the consciousness, which seemingly brought about the need for a miracle. Consciousness, our personal consciousness, sets the stage of our perception. Our personal consciousness is only part of the equation playing out in our life. We are influenced by universal consciousness and perhaps the collective consciousness of our family and tribe. All of this consciousness is not about being conscious of things or something, but rather being conscious of the consciousness unfolding around us. It is impossible for the human mind to fully embrace and comprehend the concept of infinity, but the overriding aspect of consciousness is indeed infinite. It is infinite, unending, ever, evenly present in all life. Infinity is perhaps the essence of all life.

To understand miracles and healing, we must first understand that the consciousness surrounding the illness must be transcended. When we look at the world, we are looking at our reflective consciousness. This is not as simple as looking into a mirror and assuming what you see is you. Reflective consciousness mirrors all of life back to us. It shows us how consciousness is unfolding around us, be it an illusion or reality.

For any healing to occur, our perception must change. Instead of seeing pain as an enemy, we must embrace it as a part of consciousness, understand it from a standpoint of consciousness. Our perceptions are changed. By this, I mean in our perception there is something more or less than Truth, God, and Consciousness. When, we are in alignment with spiritual law (Truth/God), we are no longer mesmerized by what appears to be illusion or ego. We have perfect recall but the angle of perception has changed. The pain, blockages, and other travesties of our ego life are moved or seen in a different light.

This is the best explanation I can give you of a miracle: what seems ordinary in life is set aside for the extraordinary experience of Truth/God. The ego life is surrendered to the spiritual law. Spiritual law is so powerful and abiding that it shines its light in every dark corner of the unconscious mind. Once the darkness is removed, the light shows the miracle in life. We have had many miracles in our life. Sometimes we did not recognize the miracle, so of course did not give gratitude to life for it. Miracles often seem so natural,. Of course! They are us, simply abiding by spiritual, law so they are natural. We don't stop to recognize the "good—God" at work.

How Surrender Works

A friend put it this way: She was diagnosed with bleeding retinas. Fearful as she walked into the specialist's office, a peace came over her and she said to her self, "If blindness is needed I will be blind. I have seen many beautiful and wonderful things and this sight will never leave me. To God I surrender my sight. It is the will of the Father (causer/Creator) of life that is the foundation of all life." Two hours later, she walked out having been told her eyes and retinas were in perfect health.

Prayer and meditation are not tools where you ask for perfect eyes or even healing. Christ said 'you ask and you pray amiss.' Prayer is about gratitude, about surrendering to the will of higher mind, God/Truth. Prayer and meditation are tools you use for a better understanding. A miracle occurred. It is important that we understand miracles and healing do happen every day. We create them by our understanding of spiritual law and our willingness to let go of the ego's needs and surrender as Job did to Truth/God being all there is no matter what our sight or perception.

If you want a miracle and need to heal, untie the box you have Truth/God in. Learn a process of aligning yourself with Truth and learn forgiveness. Embrace what is in your life, no matter what the appearance, for it is all Truth. Even the illusion is Truth misperceived.

We must all take responsibility for our emotional, physical, and not least, our spiritual health. Our emotional and physical health are direct reflections of our spiritual wellbeing. If we are not working from a base of Truth, knowing we are a spiritual, being we will suffer. We don't ask to become ill, but the causers lay deep within our unconscious mind and the silly fantasy games we play each day. We can do this we can make a miracle in this world.

CHAPTER TWELVE　　　　　　　　　　HEALING

What Keeps Me From Surrendering?
Notes

"When you struggle with your partner, you are struggling with yourself. Every fault you see in them touches a denied weakness in yourself."

~Deepak Chopra

Chapter 13

Relationships
Being Intimate

Every association is a relationship. Understanding your roles in relationships can lead to a deeper understanding of our spiritual nature. Most of our longing for a relationship is the longing for intimacy, a longing to reside in a sacred space with another. All relationships can be intimate. This means you are authentic in a relationship, not playing a role, but willing to be emotionally and spiritually naked with another. You are connecting spirit-to-spirit. Each connection, from the clerk in a store to our mates, is emotional in nature.

We seek emotional connections similar to the way we seek food containing the essential vitamins and minerals needed for our health. Intimacy (this spiritual relationship) is a primal need in our system. It is perhaps more primal than sex itself. Perhaps Maslow missed the importance of intimacy in his hierarchy of needs. The need for intimacy should follow the needs for air, water, food, and safety. Intimacy is a survival need in our unconscious mind. We often seek to satisfy this need through sexual coupling. If not through sex, how do we express intimacy in our daily lives? Once we have touched the spirit of another with our spirit, the relationship becomes one of love. Perhaps not romantic love, but love nonetheless. If we understand this, the relationship can be authentic. This means we understand it is divine and sacred in nature.

True intimacy and it's sacredness are created in a state of absolute Truth/Love. We all have loved and do love many people. Love is absolute no matter what the emotional attachment. It is eternal and the very basis of all creation. Our focus of love may change, but love is eternal. Once we recognize we love an individual, this love is not taken from us, but remains a part of our psyche and consciousness throughout eternity.

Most of our emotional behavior is based on need. We respond emotionally to situations and people because of our needs, or what our mind feels is needed for survival. Some of these needs are archetypical in nature. That is, they are symbols, seeded deep in our unconscious mind, and

Chapter Thirteen — Relationships

universal in their meanings. The concept of love or saying 'I love you' is in every culture in the world. Of course, it takes on different meanings and uses according to the social ideation of the individual. Just as the concept of housing or shelter is common throughout our world, so is the concept of love. From an anthropological standpoint, this would mean the concept of love is as important for survival as shelter. Survival needs attend to the ongoing physical life of an individual and their wellbeing.

At the moment of birth we begin building a sacred intimacy with our mother, and later with those who would care for us and love us. Nothing teaches a parent more about love than those first few moments after birth, seeing the life they have nurtured, and brought into manifestation. What is love? An emotional attachment seems an inadequate definition for what appears to be a part of our human survival. Saying 'I love you' must mean 'I need you in some manner for my continuing survival. I need not to feel separate. I want to be intimate in some manner with you.'

We know, for most people, separation and the lack of intimacy for long periods-of-time causes havoc in life. It even leads to a break down in our immune system. Without intimacy, we loose our connection to our body and find it hard to stay present and alert. Saying 'I love you' produces a connection of emotional intimacy and an acknowledgment of existence on a common emotional plane. It is as needed as fruit and vegetables in our diet to keep us healthy. Saying 'I love you' is saying 'I recognize your existence; I am willing to communicate with you. I am willing to allow you to know me.' When we tell our children 'I love you,' we are saying 'I know you, feel connected to you, and I know you feel the connection and can know me.' The importance of these simple words carries impacts we can't begin to describe. Saying 'I love you' cures, heals, and produces joy. It cannot be said too much, for the very word 'love' creates a vibration in our being, which neutralizes fear, hate, and insanity.

Every stage of a relationship, specially a romantic one, is a role playing, a game of attraction. You try to be at your best in every area. It is a common thing to do. You assume this is the one who is going to make you happy, make you feel special. In turn, you will play the part of who he or she wants you to be. You make a mental agreement and you keep playing this part.

You make a mental agreement and you keep playing this part. The acting cannot be permanent. Sooner or later, you will relax, especially when you start living together. When the cover-up is over what is left is the you as you are, unmasked, with the unfulfilled self.

Chapter Thirteen Relationships

You have put your true self on the shelf for a while, but now it wants to be, and wants to be fulfilled. You don't know each other. Many times, we start a relationship by being addicted to the image the other presents to us, but this is not love. Love exists when our spirits touch another in a sacred space. This sacred space demands there be no pretending or masks. To enter into love, as love, you drop all of the roles you play and accept that you are the embodiment of love.

If you are looking for the perfect person and you will never find it. Love has nothing to do with finding love. Love already is love. It needs no manipulation, role-playing, or pretense. It needs nothing. All you need to do is to accept love and let it flow. Once two people feel they love each other, they usually begin with demands. The demands and expectations stop the natural flow of love. Release yourself and your loved one from the roles and demands of old beliefs and society's idea of a what relationship should be.

Each of us wants to be with a super-human. The media and society's influences take hold of us early. Your personal references are based on a program that is set to fail, but there is another option, a challenging one, the only one that can work; it is about creating a new and spontaneous life together, based on a moment-to-moment presence.

One of the clients I consult with was using a vision board—a concept used by many well-known experts on self-improvement. This is a very old kind of visualization used by many early metaphysicians. To me, this is absurd, because most people who rely on this concept are looking outside of the their consciousness. What we manifest comes from within our consciousness, our thinking. Using images from newspapers and magazines, this client had cut out pictures of James Bond, a yacht, designer clothes, accessories, a Rolls Royce, and money. These paper clippings where attached to this board, hanging on the wall of her living room, where she would go to it everyday, just like a shrine, and envision these things to materialize in her life.

There was nothing on this board on spirituality, nothing on self-love or love, period. Love and the true essence of life can't be stored on a wallboard: it is only stored in the heart and soul. Worldly possessions don't make us happy. Possessions can't fill the void we feel when we don't understand our purpose and meaning.

Soul Mate

You have put your true self on the shelf for a while, but now it wants to be and wants to be fulfilled. You are looking for the perfect person and you will never find it. Love has nothing to do with love, love is already love. It needs no manipulation, role-playing, or change. It needs nothing.

All you need to do is to accept and let it flow. To be in an authentic relationship you need to create a state of sacredness, a place specifically for this is relationship. There is no need to find a soul mate, for every relationship is a soul mate relationship. We all share one soul and the essence of our being.

The paradox of wanting love and intimacy, and fearing it, is the point where we can remember our true being. The paradox in itself puts our ego to sleep long enough for the higher consciousness— the Truth, the God within— to come forth, producing an epiphany or change of mind, literally shifting the whole consciousness. In turn, this shift brings about a new perception of love and intimacy in our life. Our experiences then will reflect this shift in consciousness.

The fear of being naked (emotionally and psychically) in the presence of our lovers ('lovers' being all of those who love us, we love, and isn't meant sexually), stems from our feelings of guilt of not being good enough for the connection. We fear our being is soiled in some manner, our thoughts of self-loathing, and guilt will be revealed to the other. We misunderstand the concept of perfection, thinking our human idea of perfection is of the Creator Source. Humanity sees perfection as the rose without the thorn. Creation says I am whole and complete and the rose is perfect, thorn and all. The perfection of being has nothing to do with physical appearance, emotional maturity, or spiritual achievement. Perfection deals with the wholeness, and completeness of Truth/God. Truth/God is whole and perfect, is all there is, and nothing else is needed. It is perfection. This is important because when we reach for perfection, we get caught in our beliefs and fears of not being worthy.

We are the effect of the Creator Source, as a book is written from the mind of the author and bread is baked from the creative aspect of a baker. What we create from our thoughts is the essence of existence. The essence of the Creator is in the progeny, be it a book, bread, or humanity. In this, we share the nature of the Creator Source: whole, complete, and perfect.

Being told we are loved and saying I love you can lower the level of fear and hormones that destroy our bodies and minds. Saying I love you says simply, I feel connected to you, I want you to love me and feel connected to me. Intimacy and love are basic survival needs. Both must be present for a sacred connection to occur between individuals.

Chapter Thirteen — Relationships

To be intimate with an individual, an idea or Truth/God we must create a sacred space. All intimacy is sacred.

How I Act Out in Relationships
Notes

"Power is of two kinds. One is obtained by the fear of punishment and the other by acts of love. Power based on love is a thousand times more effective and permanent then the one derived from fear of punishment."

~Mahatma Gandhi

Chapter 14

Power

Power is extremely seductive. Humanity has the idea that power keeps us safe, and aids in our basic survival. It appears we see power as a god-like quality. The more power we have, the closer to being a god we feel we are.

Power on a physical plane of existence is temporal. The seduction of power feeds the ego. When we assume a god-like stance with power, we loose sight of our compassion and empathic natures. We act from a temporal plane, making judgments and decisions that are less than stellar. The ego would have you believe all of your decisions and judgments are worthy. You are, according to the ego, infallible.

Temporal power is addictive and illusive. The ego is its source. Our egos work from a survival mode. This means it is always thinking it will not survive and tries to do what it thinks it needs to do to survive. This kind of consciousness puts self-interest above the good for all actions an awakened individual will have.

Ego has many faces and often is not easily detectable. Our egos have all the power as we sleepwalk through our life. When we awaken to our true power and identity, we see clearly. It is like a light being turned on in a darkened room. We are no longer stumbling around and tripping over the furniture. The ego rules most lives. To be under the influence of the ego is like driving on a dark road with your lights off. It gives a false feeling of importance, superiority or sense of belonging. In actuality, it is fear that makes you hold on to the ego. Fear of failure, being hurt, dying, and losing your identity. Some people, even in their illness, are under the influence of ego. It is during sickness they get attention from others which otherwise they would not. It is rare for the majority of humans to live their lives without the influence of the ego.

Authentic Power

The only real power any of us have is consciousness aware of consciousness. Huge amounts of power are released, untold light, and splendor when we embrace our true-identity, spirit. Knowing our true-identity, understanding we are of spirit and releasing ourselves from false beliefs, releases us from the dark night and pain of separation.

Authentic power happens only to those who have awakened to Truth. You know these people; they are the miracle workers, the compassionate ones, and those who create a better life for everyone. Authentic power does not seek power or fame, nor is it greedy. It is there when needed; it is from a divine source.

When you realize the ego is an illusory identity, it quickly dissolves. Authentic power is the power that does not need to be fueled by ego. This power is of divine source and it is already part of us. It is the original seed you and I have in our DNA imprint. It is our inherited right to use this divine power, but it cannot manifest until we let go of our false identity. Your true-identity is not something you need to seek. Like Truth/God it is already present. Turn within to find yourself, for nothing exists outside of your consciousness.

You ask, "What do I need to think about to get it?" The answer is, "On the contrary, you need not to think." You already exist, don't you? This in itself tells you if you exist—you must have come from something. This something is the Creator of life. You are part of It, you are this which created you, and you have what It has. You are this already. There is nothing to think; nothing to say; nothing to do. All there is, is to be. Embrace humanity as your brothers and sisters of spirit.

A person who has authentic power is a teacher and leader to those around them. When in authentic power an individual safeguards the life and happiness of all. They exhibit the ways of love for all to see. They understand and speak the truth. They are compassionate and empathetic in their actions and thinking. They consciously set out to make their life (and all those whose lives they touch) peaceful, beautiful, and happy. They show respect for all existence. Those who call on divine source and use authentic power make sure that each project is in service of love. The actions they take make spiritual energy, a force that can be used by all, and for the betterment of humanity.

CHAPTER FOURTEEN — POWER

How I Would Use Power
Notes

"Our intention creates our reality."

~Wayne Dyer

Chapter 15

Create Your Own Reality

All of the accumulated information and experiences you carry, what are you going to do with it all? Are you still living the old experiences? Are you repeating patterns? Let me tell you, all of what you have experienced, and what's in your memory, can be used in two ways. One way is you can choose to be lazy and just keep on repeating the same experiences, without creativity, innovation, advancement, and newness. You can stay in the illusion, or you have another choice: to create a never-before-experienced life and your own reality.

Hypnotic Reality

Each of us has written a contract with our idea of reality. Each day our contract plays itself out in our life. The problem with these contracts is they were not written with reality but with fantasy, illusion, and beliefs of what reality is. The actuality that we create out of beliefs is an experience we live with daily. We see, feel, taste, hear, and speak our beliefs every moment. Only when we stay present in the NOW moment do we suspend our beliefs and fantasy reality. Just because something appears in our memory does not make it so. We believe that the sky is blue, grass is green, a wall is solid, and time exists. In fact, all of these are beliefs. They are agreed upon beliefs, but beliefs and illusions nonetheless. At anytime we can agree to change our beliefs. Hypnotists have shown this on stage. They plant a belief in the mind of the subject and the subject will act accordingly.

Our experiences and actions are based on a set of beliefs. Our belief system is hypnotic, filled with fears, anxiety, fantasy, illusion, suffering, and pain. Every moment you remain present in the now, aware of your true identity, you break through this hypnotic state. Human beings have a wonderful sensual self. We use all of our senses in pleasure and pain. The pull of the senses is so great we allow ourselves to be drawn into them and hypnotized by what they are seemingly reporting. Like a mirage in a hot desert, we see water and an oasis when none exists.

We don't make a conscious choice on how we will identify ourselves. As children, the long process begins. We are, all at once, naughty, good, a student, the son or daughter of our mothers and fathers. The labels continue. Out of these labels, we build our identity. We accept these labels as a definition of our identity. With the labels come prescribed kinds of behavior. By feeding those behaviors, slowly we sign contracts that define our experience.

We have signed a contract with a dream state reality. We believe we are the labels and the labels become our identity.

Your existence is not in parts, but rather a whole, using many characteristics in your expression and manifestation. This means, even if a label were to be true, it would not be you. Our being remains whole and is not split into parts or pieces. When you say I AM you are saying I AM I and this exists in this moment of NOW because it is the only moment, it is infinite. Being infinite, it is whole and complete. The experience of whole identity and reality can't be rationalized. It can't be intellectualized. You can only experience it and know it. When you experienced the infinity of your identity, you have experienced the alpha and omega of being.

You are, at this moment, beginning to rewrite your contract with reality. Inhale slowly, bringing in fresh knowing and understanding of your being. Stay centered and in this moment. Examine the labels you have accepted as your reality. Why not leave them outside the room for a moment and experience your being unencumbered by anything other than infinite being knowing, itself as consciousness. As you exhale, let all the labels that are no longer needed go. That which is not needed is relinquished to the nothingness from which it came, like 2+2=5 goes once we understand 2+2=4.

When you are finished, you will feel taller, lighter, clear, and deliciously aware of life all around you. In this moment of NOW you will know your true identity and reality. You can, right this moment, rewrite your contract with reality by identifying yourself as I AM I, or consciousness aware of itself as consciousness.

Releasing The Dreams

Our experiential dream state is built on a series of patterns and symbols constructed out of the beliefs we hold. Patterns are those ideas and concepts which are repeated in our consciousness. We have patterns of behavior, understanding, and dreams. Patterns have pre-patterns, which often alert us to a coming repeated pattern. Within the secrets of the patterns, we find the puzzle pieces of our life. Understanding the patterns in our lives helps us know when we are in a dream state. Where you see a pattern, there you will find a dream state and illusion of existence. Life seems very real in a dream state.

Chapter Fifteen — Reality

Part of the contract we have written with our beliefs and unconscious exist in these patterns within the dream.

To rewrite your contract with reality you must begin to see the patterns and their connections. You must see how the symbols play out. To do this, stay in the present moment. When you stay present in the NOW you become lucid. In a lucid state, you can watch the dream state play out in an objective manner. The patterns reveal themselves when you are lucid. When you remain lucid in the NOW you become consciousness aware of consciousness. In this one eternal moment, you can release yourself from the patterns, symbols, and old identity. You set yourself free from the old patterns of your now lucid state of awareness. In this moment, you know you have always been consciousness aware of consciousness. At this moment of release, the splendor you have always been will come forth.

As you inhale, bring light and lucidity into your being. As you stay present, notice the patterns in your life. Recognize the limiting patterns of behavior and identity. As you exhale, allow these dream states to dissipate and leave your being.

Release each one that reveals itself to you. Release it knowing that you are awareness, consciousness, I AM I. It is in this state of lucid awareness that you can rewrite your contract with reality.

Making New Symbols

Words, dreams, and life are all symbolic. Words have no meaning other than the significance we give them. Dreams are the same way. Their importance is only in our thinking. An illusion has no meaning other than the meaning assigned by you. Before we gave a word importance, it was nothing more than a sound; air going over our larynx and out our mouth. Language is an agreed upon meaning by a group who use the particular sounds. For instance, the word green means green not because the word means green, but because we have agreed upon that particular sound meaning the word green.

Meanings, experiences, and dreams are all stored as symbols in our memory. When you stay present and in the NOW state of being, old meanings of symbols are automatically removed from your consciousness. You can clear symbols of fear aggression, and you can let go of the symbols of hurt, pain, and guilt. You do this by simply staying present and recognizing your true-identity as awareness, consciousness. As you stay present in the moment of NOW you will recognize anytime you could have let go of the symbols of the past. In this moment, the past is a dream the only reality is this moment, it is the only time we have. The longer you remain present in this moment the more time you spend rewriting your contracts. Like waking up from a dream the longer you are awake the more the dream fades and the reality of the moment takes over.

In your meditations and times of contemplation, identify those symbols of the past that no longer serve you. Let them go as you exhale and inhale the now as I AM I The dream fades and the reality of the moment takes over.

Keeping Promises

It is easy to become trapped in your dream state. Fantasy is very addictive. Fantasy offers a promise, but the promise is like the oasis, just another mirage. Becoming lucid takes you deeper into conscious awareness of reality. When you accept the essence of life in this moment, you are freed from the addiction of delusion and a new reality is formed. You could say, as of this moment, you have returned to the reality which has always has been.

Many times in our life, we will write contracts with others. One of the characteristics of a contract is that you promise a certain deed or behavior for a reward or benefit of some sort. Most of the time, we are not aware of what we are contracting for. It looks good, seems right, and always seems like it is what we want. Contracts that are written in a dream state are made of illusion. No matter what they promise, they are nothing more than a whiff of imagination, an illusion. The only real contract is the contract you make by accepting this moment. By accepting this moment, that which is so, you have made a contract with reality. You have made a contract with yourself as the causer of your consciousness. The only real promise any of us have is that we are consciousness aware of consciousness. Quietly exhale the illusion and inhale the promise of consciousness. Let go of the dream state contracts as you rewrite your reality as consciousness aware of itself as consciousness. You are no longer consciousness aware of things and dreams, but rather consciousness aware as consciousness.

Our Creation

Choose not to believe the things you think about are It. They are not It! Enjoy the process of creation. Be imaginative and daring in your heart and mind. Allow your thoughts to be free of the dangerous triumvirate of "should," "would," and "could." Revel and rebel. Do not permit anything negative to guide your thoughts. Once you have begun to think for yourself, the process will get easier. After all, you are bucking a lifetime of misinformation. It is your absolute prerogative to think what you choose. Position yourself firmly behind the wheel and think autonomously. It's your road, your reality, and your life. You can absolutely make whatever of it you desire.

My Realities That Manifest

"I know but one freedom and that is the freedom of the mind."

~Antoine De Saint-Exupery

Chapter 16

Responsibility Is Freedom

Appreciate the ability you possess to handle any challenge you may face on your life journey. You are fully capable. You don't have to wait for assistance or instruction from anyone else or ask permission to live your dreams. Many of us learned as children to do what we were told and waited for permission before moving forward. We entered a school, which indoctrinated us into a way in which we view achievement. We graduate from one level to the next and waited for approval before moving forward. We may learn to excel within a similar framework, in a career where our tasks are dictated for us.

Waiting for permission or guidance from someone else could be a familiar habit. You hold the brush that will paint the picture of your life story. You can seek advice or assistance from friends and family but you are the only one who can search for just the right colors to fill your life's canvas. As much as others may care, they are just not capable of living your life for you. Don't blame others in your life for your failures. This disempowers you. Nobody is taking advantage of you—they are just focused on the opportunities that life presents for them, to complete their own journey. You must do the same.

Finding fault with circumstances, other people, or anything else is a way to avoid responsibility and sidestep the work you have to complete. Once you realize responsibility is a blessing not a burden, you suddenly have access to a whole new world. By accepting responsibility for everything, which happens in your life, you now have the freedom to choose any life you desire. Fill the canvas with any form. Splash it with colors that bring you joy. Don't be afraid of making a mistake.

We are consciousness/Truth and a manifestation of the Creator source. We are more than nature, or what appears to us through our senses. Living in a cloven consciousness state we are acutely aware of good and evil, or we can destroy in hate and revenge or we can invent and create in great harmony and absolute love. In our humanity, there is a freedom of inventive and creative forces.

Chapter Sixteen — Responsibility

There is no freedom in the essence of our being. We cannot choose to *not* be consciousness, Truth, the manifestation of the Creator Source. However, within our humanity there is a freedom of inventiveness and creativity. In this,energy and consciousness we can either create harmonious, beautiful, and loving ideas, or we can invent and create ideas that are used for destruction and tyranny. We are free to choose the intent we use in our inventiveness and creativity. We can choose our own intention and how we express our freedom and liberty. We can move beyond the fear/aggression ego drives to choose an experience as consciousness.

No law, no tyrannical force, can dictate to you intention or morality. Moral or immoral, ethical or wrong, good and evil. These are all interior concepts a person who intends consciousness discovers. Freedom is within our consciousness. Circumstances and government can neither take it nor bestow it. Freedom of intention is inherent within the core of our humanity.

Your purpose, passion, and desire can never be taken from you. Your survival is not dependent on greed or destruction of another's well being but on your own intention and discovery of the limitless freedom in consciousness.

The paradox presented by freedom is that we have no freedom to be other than consciousness in the expression of the nature of reality and yet we have all freedom to choose. Within the paradox of freedom/no freedom is the answer to all life.

The Secret of Freedom

With individuality, you create independence and self-reliance by taking responsibility for your actions and their consequences. To be free, you have to have the power to decide things for yourself, take responsibility for your life, your actions, and your decisions. You cannot give that responsibility to someone else and be free. You should have the freedom and the power to choose your own way and not have it decided for you by others who might think they know what is best for society, but not necessarily, what is best for you.

Only you know what is best for you inside yourself! So, you have the power to become the best you can be. Authentic power is to be able to fulfill your own hopes and dreams for today and the future. The secret of freedom is knowing your inner spirit and desires. Freedom is an attitude and willingness to be responsible for your actions and inactions.

Chapter Sixteen — Responsibility

Quest for Freedom

It has been my experience that freedom and the need for freedom happen in everyone's life once they achieved a certain level of survival and competency in their day-to-day activities. Inherent in the human spirit is the drive to defy rules and rulers, to rebel against the constraints imposed on it by authority figures, society, and the limits of its own nature. This drive is not an aberration, nor does it run contrary to the human nature's intrinsic loyalty to and seeking of higher ideals. Each of us carries a sense of higher self, which is utterly free of all limitation and definition, in this we posses the desire-and potential-for an utterly free and unconstrained existence. Only, as a free beings, has humanity realized its highest potentials in the sciences, the arts, and the quest to understand and know ourselves. All freedom begins with an inner desire. No matter what our circumstances, our nationality, or our education, we must look within to free ourselves. Trust in the limitless potential you have to be creative, and happy. Share with others in trust. Have confidence.

Extraordinary Understanding

We know that to reach a state of higher Source, God TRUTH, we must first understand the existence. That which is so about the nature of reality— Truth—is always so, always there. So the first questions that come to me are these: Why aren't we participating in this Truth as Truth? What keeps us from experiencing this?'

What blocks us from this experience? There are of course many things, which block us from an experience of Truth and God. Personal blocks of course reside in us as man-state fears and wants. But, beyond these, there are other blocks, which come from a misunderstanding of basic principles. To understand what these blocks are we must start by how we reach this source, this state of existence.

We reach Truth by extraordinary thought and understanding. That which is ordinary cannot understand the existence of Truth as all there is. We must reach beyond our egos and fears for something much greater. Truth is found in our extraordinary sense of self. When we reach for what is beyond our chrysalis seeking something greater than what we know, we find the idea of trust.

Trust is an act of emotion and logic. We trust the car will stop at the red light. This is a logical act of trust. We want our friends not to betray our openness and to be loyal. This is an act of emotional trust.

If in an act of logical trust, the car goes through

Chapter Sixteen — Responsibility

the light, we look for facts and data telling us how this has happened. Did the brakes fail? Was there another mitigating factor? Logically, it is where you have assessed the probabilities of gain and loss, calculating expected utility based on hard performance data, and concluded the person in question will behave in a predictable manner.

What about emotional trust? How do we know about it and what part does it play in our reaching God? Truth? In practice, trust is a bit of both. I trust you because I have experienced your trustworthiness and because I have faith in human nature. How do I trust the path I am on is the right path? How do I know I will survive? How do I trust God, Truth enough to trust in a state of surrender? Can I be safe enough to surrender my ego and will? Can I trust enough in my surrender to experience the totality of Truth?

None of these are easy questions to answer nor are the questions about trust quickly answered. Trust in relation to God and Truth is an emotional act. There is nothing logical about the experience of God and Truth. There are no facts you can collect on the trustworthiness of Truth unless you have had an experience. So how do you trust Truth? Trust God?

Sitting quietly, exhale ordinary thoughts about trust and betrayal. Inhale the consciousness of the primary causer, consciousness, formlessness manifesting infinitely. Exhale the ego's resistance to surrendering to Truth, Spirit, and God. Inhale the consciousness of trust and knowing. Do this until you feel comfortable with the idea of surrendering your ego. The ego mind will quiet. God, Consciousness, and Truth are an experience, which breaks through the ordinary thoughts to extraordinary understanding of the nature of reality.

The Will of Ego

Logic, intellect, or emotions cannot lead you to a place of peace of knowing and experiencing God and Truth. You get there by surrendering will and ego. And this takes trust in your self. Trust that can withstand the battering and nagging of the ego. Ego says such things as 'yeah right, *this* is going to work' and your will builds a wall. You say 'no, not me, not this time.' We become exhausted from dealing with our ego and will.

The energy of Truth and God is so great the polarity of the ego and will sets up a mighty pull on our emotional and mental state. The fears we experience are in direct proportion to absolute love available as God and Truth. The darkness we feel before a revelation is proportionate to the light of understanding available to us, the silence equals the whispers of God available to us. But, none of this makes sense in man state thinking, none of this satisfies the ego and will. In an act of surrendering the will and ego, we find trust. We learn trust is a state of acceptance of our divine nature and act of extraordinary experience of ourselves. We are no longer adrift in a friendless Universe but a member of a great choir, singing hosanna unto the presence of Truth and nothing else. Trust teaches us that Truth is all there is without alpha and omega. God created all there is. If Truth is all there is how can there be anything outside of God? All else is fantasy, illusion, and puppet shows set up by our ego and will.

Trust appears when we surrender our ordinary thoughts about life for an extraordinary experience of trusting that Truth is all there is.

Risk

Trust is an attitude we have toward another or an idea. Trust is a primary component to relationships that have meaning and purpose in our lives. Both parties must be trustworthy. But if you are talking about a relationship with Truth, God, and consciousness how do you know the other is trustworthy? Trust comes with a certain risk, and it can be dangerous. There is always the risk of betrayal of trust, and the loss of self-respect. In human relationships we learn to trust, we must cultivate the attitude necessary for it to occur.

Because trust involves risk, it is also dangerous. Others can choose to act as trustworthy and fulfill the actions necessary or not. Placing our trust in the other we risk loosing what we are entrusting to another, including our self-respect.

The dominant paradigm of trust is interpersonal. It is a human idea, a human way of dealing with primary energy such as God, Consciousness, and Truth. Truth or axiomatic concepts, universal and natural principles present no emotion. But to form an intimate relationship a trusting relationship we must build an attitude, which trusts without any evidence other than consistency and irrefutable concepts or principles. The relationship we form is human in nature but axiomatic in action. The risk and danger to us is we may trust something that is not so. Trust in divine mind, God, Truth, and Consciousness is not a human act, no matter how it appears it is an act of conscious awareness of the primary energy of life. Trust is an intentional surrendering of our intellect and reason to something that is much greater and indefinable. The ego causes the fear of what cannot be known by the intellect. Trust is an act of Consciousness.

Vulnerability

In an act of trust, you must be willing to be vulnerable to the (person, Truth, God, consciousness) actions. There is an unspoken expectation the acts committed will be important to the person who is trusting. This trust is given regardless of the ability to control outcomes or monitor the situation.

To build a relationship of any sort with Truth, God, Consciousness, or another person requires the building of trust. Trust in relationships is the expectancy of people that they can rely on your word. It is built through integrity and consistency. If you are to trust Truth, God, and Consciousness then you must understand the axiomatic principles involved. Universal or natural principles are always consistent. They are ever evenly present through out the Universe.

Becoming vulnerable surrendering to truth in an act of trust takes a certain amount of courage. In some cases, it is like leaping a chasm with what is called blind faith. We feel by controlling our will we are safe. We fear betrayal, which is the breaking of trust.

To be vulnerable to Truth, God, and Consciousness we must be willing to be influenced. That is when we surrender our will and become vulnerable we are open to the influence and power of higher source, Truth, God, and Consciousness. When we are practicing intentional consciousness, we are practicing acts of surrender, surrendering our will and ego for something much greater. To have trust we must release our fears and lack of self-trust to a greater idea, Truth. Trust is not logical from a human way of thinking. It is not useful nor is it safe. Human thinking seeks control, but in trusting your higher source,

Truth and God you must step over the edge of the cliff, into the circle of fire, you must leap into sanity. You must be vulnerable to God, Truth, and Consciousness and leap into sanity.

Reflective Empathy

Empathy is a valued skill attitude needed in building trust in human relationships. It helps us understand why and how others are reacting to situations, and adds information to our data gathering and decisions. Our daily life reflects our consciousness. Attitudes, habits, and beliefs play out in our relationships. This includes our relationships with Consciousness, Truth, and God.

The reflective aspect of life allows us to have a view of consciousness beyond what our ego would want us to see. Our ability to trust another is directly related to our perception of the integrity and consistency of another. This is the same with trusting God, Truth, and Consciousness. If our perception is one where we see the consistency of universal and natural law in Consciousness,

Chapter Sixteen — Responsibility

Truth and God we will be able to trust in an act of surrendering our ego will.

As we learn to observe with empathy the unfolding of life around us, we are practicing a skill we need to be able to trust others and ourselves. It is important to cultivate skills such as empathy, listening, and staying present to build trust in all relationships.

Choices

If we understand how the mind works and how our life reflects from the subconscious, we realize freedom is indeed a degree. No one is ever entirely objective and free from beliefs imposed by society, family, and our cultures. These are deeply ingrained in us and even the most persistent accolade accomplishes goals by degrees. It is never 100% hot or cold.

Each step we take to cut a cord to a belief we are that much freer and able to exercise true free will and choice. Abraham Maslow states, in his hierarchy of needs, that we must first fulfill our survival, food, water, air, and safety, before we can move forward to determining our course of actions based on intellectual and spiritual needs.

We are at the core human. No manner of denial or praying will free us from certain needs and drives. We can make more aware, conscious, choices. We can exercise our ethics and moral choices based on freedom, and spiritual good that benefits all. We are still saddled with subconscious beliefs, drives, and fears that influence us, no matter how subtle. We are subjective in nature. Nothing can make us purely objective and free from constraints of beliefs and our cultural inculcations. It is again a matter of degrees.

It is this humanity of subjectivity, which eventually leads us to understand the ontological concept of a divinity held within each life force. Perhaps it is the God of Abraham in the Bible, or Buddha, but we each have this supra consciousness, pure, unadulterated. In our humanity we realize this. We choose to be free, not because our government allows this, because this supra consciousness pushes forth to be known and revealed.

This push to unfold, to reach beyond, to be known, is the force that moves us forward in our life to know life differently to understand purpose and to understand ideas such as freedom, choice, and free will. To the degree we are aware of this inner force is the degree we are willing to seek openly that which is the spirit of being. Choices are not choices unless you know yourself well enough to know why you choose, life partners, food, career and many other significant ar-

CHAPTER SIXTEEN   RESPONSIBILITY

eas in your life. Even then, the hidden paradigms of the subconscious mind form the structure of your choices in ways we don't understand or even notice. To choose freely is to understand why you are choosing, and to understand the consequences of choosing.

Freedom can neither be given nor taken. It is not a matter of laws or government. It is how we view life. Even in the darkest prison, we have freedom of thought and to grow spiritually. Freedom, no matter how confining our circumstances, is a matter of acceptance of the idea, that our lives are not limited by our senses or our beliefs. Dictators and suppressive leadership come about out of our fears and security/survival needs. Once we understand that freedom is as much an inner choice as the flavor of our favorite ice cream, we will become free to exist in new ways.

To be conscious is about freeing the inner being to explore freedom. To make choices that are constructive rather than destructive. To intend freedom and choice is to make a conscious choice to break the bonds that keep you shackled to ideas, beliefs, and cultural programming, which limit your very existence and experience.

Am I Free?
Notes

Chapter Sixteen — Responsibility

Where I Need To Understand Responsibility
Notes

"By persisting in your path, though you forfeit the little, you gain the great."

~Ralph Waldo Emerson

Chapter 17

Destiny

Fortitude, determination, tenacity, diligence, and persistence are words that apply to those who work the limit. They have learned there is always a solution to the puzzle or the problem before them. They succeed by being tenacious and persistent until the problem is solved.

Our persistence should go beyond just solving problems. We need to be persistent about how we work on our destiny and purpose. Those who succeed know giving an idea one try is not enough. It often takes many tries to make it all work. The repeated focusing on a project and the tenacious ability to stick it out pays off. Like the story of the tortoise and the hare, the persistence of the tortoise won him the race. Our persistence will win our personal race. Embrace your destiny and purpose, be persistent, stay tenacious to your goals. Find delight with each new piece of your puzzle you find and encounter.

Every moment of every day is the only moment in time and your persistent focusing in the moment will bring you closer to fulfilling the destiny you have chosen. If you feel you lack tenaciousness or persistence, assume the attribute. Mimic someone who has the attribute. Your future is yours to take. Make this the day you begin the journey. All that is needed will be presented to you along the path you choose. Stay alert to opportunity, stay aware of movement around you, and have fortitude for what you seek lies on the path you walk.

Destiny and Belief

Know life holds some truly magical moments for you. These moments are when you see your beliefs come to life. Like a child, your inquisitive nature has you uncovering many things. When you know and start believing anything and everything is possible, many things will happen around you. These special moments are what I call 'Aha!' or 'Eureka!' (literally: 'I have found it!') moments. It is when patterns of beliefs and our purpose are so clear to us, so magical, we wonder why we have not seen them in this manner before.

Our beliefs form our destiny. If we believe we

can, we do what we believe. This is what we play out on our journey to our purpose. Research shows us if children believe they are loved and intelligent, they will do well in school and in life. If they believe no one loves them, and they are dumb, they fail time and again at the simplest of activities.

In fact, we know even the belief of a teacher effects how the student will learn and act in class. What are your beliefs? If your goals and destiny seem not so clear perhaps it is the beliefs you carry, the inner dialogue handed to you from parents, teachers, and lovers. What are you thinking about yourself? What are you thinking about your purpose? What are you thinking about your destiny?

Each person has special moments, though sometimes they feel a bit elusive. Grab them and hold onto them. The next time you feel down on your abilities and self, remember that magic feeling of being on top, because it is this belief that brings you to the top for once and all. Your destiny, your purpose fulfilled is just around the corner, grab it every piece of it when you see it.

Get Out Of Hell Free Card

Heaven and hell do exist. Heaven is when you feel peace, joy, and love. Hell exists when you feel judgment, fear, and resentment. Each of these is available to you at any moment. Your entrance into these states is a matter of personal choice. You get to choose at any moment-in-time where you want to dwell. Most of us make a knee jerk reaction when a bothersome person engages us. We are immediately sent into a degree of hell, depending on our feelings toward the person. If you have learned to be self-observant, you can go beyond these reactions, quiet your mind and make the decision not to be upset. This state of detachment comes after practice. Finding your triggers, watching yourself react, eventually you can stop the reaction before it begins. In your thinking, you realize the reaction is not worth disturbing your sense of peace and joy.

There is in fact a physical reality, but you are the one that gives it meaning and purpose. You can turn it into a hell or think of it in terms of peace and joy. You can reside in absolute love as a vessel of love, or you can take on paranoia and fear, and live in hell.

The challenge of spiritual study is being able to find the spiritual reality in our physical one. As you awaken to your nakedness, (free of roles in consciousness) you find you are free of judgment, and grasping desires. This naked consciousness must come to terms with the experiences, memories, and physics of the world we reside in. We might be full of holes molecularly, but a brick is still going to break our toe if it falls on us.

For me, part of the joy of heaven is having productive relationships. By this, I mean relationships that are harmonious and fulfilling. It is important to not get too spacey with all we have been talking about. Good communication with others helps set our consciousness in a space where we are free of the existential void. Being free of the existential void means we are no longer vacant in our purpose in life. Half of all clients you find in a psychologist's office suffer from lack of purpose and meaning in their life. To find purpose and meaning we must seek freedom from our old beliefs and paradigms.

I believe spiritual awareness creates in each of us a deeper reality of our responsibility to not cause suffering in others. This does not mean we aren't responsible for our reactions, it means there are spiritual, moral, and ethical concepts, which help us form a more unified and peaceful world.

Here are some ideas that will help you get your free card to get out of hell.

1) Embrace the idea of Oneness, one mind, and consciousness. There is one consciousness, and as we accept this oneness, the separation of Spirit and Being is lessened. Judgmental thinking

causes separation and suffering, usually our own.

2) Daily, take an inward journey. In this state of self-reflection, quiet the ego mind's chattering. Allow yourself to start viewing the rush your ego gets as your daily film, and the roles you are acting, play out. Empty out all of the ego's ideas. Start by exhaling the stress and chatter. Sitting quietly inhale the peace, and joy that is naturally yours. Take a meditation class. Meditation works for millions of people.

3) At every turn, practice compassion. Compassion is essential: it brings you closer to others and lessens feelings of alienation. We are in this together. There is no peace until there is peace for everyone. The smallest act of compassion reverberates throughout the Universe. Like a pebble in a pond, the waves are felt at the very edges.

4) Love deeply and with meaning. This does not mean you must be romantic, but you find love in everything. Finding beauty in all life honors the spirit of all. Love and compassion are contagious. The more they are used, the more they are used!

5) Participate in a spiritual community that allows you to give and receive love. A spiritual community is reflective and supportive. Our work as spiritual beings starts with self, embracing the teachings, the teacher within (often reflective

our spiritual community leader), then finally the school or community and the world. Eventually we see the world as our spiritual community.

6) Stay positive in your thinking and feelings, which reflecting this positivity to all. Be in the love. Stay in touch with your loving consciousness. Don't allow the news and other things to fill your head.

7) Give gratitude to the higher self, the father within every day. Start your day with gratitude and end it with gratitude. The very idea that you can be grateful for the love you have is wonderful. This is your get out of hell free card, loving awareness that practices compassion and self-awareness.

Tony Almeida
May 2012

Desire

I stand on the edge of my Universe. I have found the cliff of insanity. Toes are wiggling over the edge in anticipation. Swirls of clouds and stars seem to appear and then drift out of sight. Winds of light sweep past churning the atmosphere into a hectic energy. My being is pulsating to unknown rhythms of creative forces.

Each new vision brings me closer to the reality I am. Slowly my hand reaches out to touch the softness of life itself. The shock of new life energy travels through my senses exploding in my mind like a cascade of eternal experiences. I am I, and none other. I am this life I have only witnessed. I am I in an exquisite moment of desire. Once more, I reach out to touch and again I find desire and experience of being. I am I.

I slowly turn to see what is around and I find again the turbulent winds of light surround me beckoning me to a new place in life. The desire of being wells up in me and I want to know the eternal experience of I am I. This desire is strong in me, driving me closer to the edge of the cliff of what feels like insanity. The fear of what will be if I step over the edge comes to my throat, but I cannot speak of this fear. All reason has left my thoughts all barriers have been surrendered. My pulsating heart will not let this rest.

Chapter Seventeen — Destiny

I have come far in this journey and know it must be completed if I am to be whole and perfect in my expression of being. More than anything, I know I want this, desire it above all else that can be. I thirst for this experience that strips me of all will and ego. Yet, I cannot tell you what it is. I cannot describe what has no description. I can only speak of what surrounds me in this moment of encounter.

As I draw back the desire to know to be is strong, I AM I comes forth again pushing me once more to the brink of chaos, of what I feel must be insanity. There is no other way, I must step over the edge of all reason, I must surrender my life for this greater pull on my being. As I look below there is great chaos, visions I cannot describe, sights, I have never seen, and sounds never heard. The fluidity of life surrounds me leaving me without form and stars to guide me in this journey.

And it has happened. The winds of light have pushed me over the edge into the pit of insanity, my throat cannot scream its fear nor my heart stop itself from pounding. The desire to know what is ahead pushes me deeper and deeper into this moment of chaos. At last I am surrendering to this that will be in my life. My being cannot comprehend what is to be it can only accept this moment of light and vision and in the moment of surrender, I accept what has always been. I am I.

I am I is known in this moment of desire. Now I know my desire has created a new reality of consciousness for me. The visions not seen are before me as consciousness aware of consciousness.

The sounds are now the songs of life itself of the reality I have created in this moment of desire. The insanity has turned into order and reason. This is life this is as consciousness. Filled with sounds of life and love, filled with understanding and the reality I am I, I am the creator of my reality, I am the creator of my awareness. Out of my desire comes consciousness aware of itself as consciousness the reality of being. I am I. As I desire so shall I create.

Take my hand and leap with me into sanity. We can do this together. We can do this with compassion and love. Take my hand as we walk the path to the stars and sun.

Love is why we exist and why we came here. Take my hand in this glorious moment of creation.

© Suzanne Deakins
When God Whispers

Chapter Seventeen — Destiny

"Character cannot be developed in ease and quiet. Only through experience of trial and suffering can the soul be strengthened, ambition inspired, and success achieved."

~Helen Keller

Afterword

I can give you all the words in the dictionary, but nothing will transform for you until you are willing to become responsible for your consciousness and change your mind. All of us suffer, most of our suffering is unnecessary, and we can overcome it. The suffering in the world is connected to our delusional cultural conditioning created by religions, governments, family, schools, and the media.

Our personal stories are all different, but each story is about who we think we are. Our egos continue to evade the light of reality, believing our mere stories are the whole of us. Personal and world suffering can be transformed when we learn to change how we think. Let us change our minds.

We suffer because we don't have those things we think we should have, because we see the world as fragile, and temporal. We suffer by continuing to choose the reality of illusion as our identity, rather than understanding that we are spirit in nature, and extraordinary in our very existence.

In this moment, your personal story is nonexistence. What our egos believe we are resides in the past, what our egos want us to become resides in the future. Our guilt and depression are over things and events, which happened in the past, or we feel anxious about what might happen or what we might not have.

It is my hope you have gained insight into your personal suffering from reading this book. The miracle of our existence is that we can create miracles by changing our thinking, by letting go of the programming of our cultures and leaders who no longer are compassionate.

Each thread you cut in gaining your freedom is like a sweater that is slowly unraveling. Slowly, one thread at a time, we will free the whole world from suffering. We are at a time of great revolution the revolution of spirit who refuses to dwell caught in guilt, pain, and suffering.

Spirit make, me an instrument of the father within. Where there is strife let me be a maker of peace. Where there is pain let me bring healing. Where there is fear let me bring love and compassion. Where there is darkness let there be eternal light. Make me an instrument...

Colophon

Titles set in OptimusPrincepes

Text set in Minion Pro
Formatted in Adobe InDesign
Printed In USA

www.onespiritpress.com
info@onespiritpress.com

This is NOT It!

www.ingramcontent.com/pod-product-compliance
Lightning Source LLC
Chambersburg PA
CBHW070537170426
43200CB00011B/2454